WHIZ QUIZ SERIES

WHO WHAT WHEN WHERE WHY

In the World of

WORLD HISTORY

by
Andy Seamans
Syndicated Columnist

illustrations by
Tom Kerr
Editorial Cartoonist

BARRON'S

To My Children . . . and Theirs

All inquiries should be addressed to:
Barron's Educational Series, Inc.
250 Wireless Boulevard
Hauppauge, New York 11788

Library of Congress Catalog Card No. 91-31563

International Standard Book No. 0-8120-4408-8

Library of Congress Cataloging-in-Publication Data
Seamans, Andy.
    Who, what, when, where, why in the world of world
history / by Andy Seamans ; with cartoon illustrations by
Tom Kerr.
        p.   cm. — (Barron's whiz quiz series)
    Summary: A collection of trivia questions and answers
about world history.
    ISBN 0-8120-4408-8
    1. World history—Miscellanea—Juvenile literature.
[1. World history—Miscellanea. 2. Questions and
answers.] I. Kerr, Tom, ill. II. Title. III. Series.
D21.S387 1991b
909—dc20   91-31563
                                                    CIP
                                                    AC

PRINTED IN THE UNITED STATES OF AMERICA
1 2 3 4   5500   9 8 7 6 5 4 3 2 1

Contents

Introduction

For those of you who are new to Barron's Whiz Quiz Series, welcome to the world of trivia. For those of you who have read some of the previously released books, welcome back.

As the title states, the subject of this book is world history, but don't expect this to be a textbook. Oh, you'll learn many interesting things about world history, but, more important, you'll have fun doing it.

We're going to test your knowledge of the wonders of world history and many of the major events leading to the present, but we're also going to quiz you on some fascinating occurrences that are not covered in your standard textbooks. In other words, you're going to be quizzed on some things you never learned in school, but which are nonetheless appealing.

When you think of history as the story of what happened to your ancestors it becomes more interesting. When you think of it as the story of why certain events of today are occurring it becomes more compelling.

Before we begin our tour through the world of history, let's set some ground rules. First of all, to paraphrase a prominent figure in modern history: Let's make this perfectly clear, this is by no means intended to be a textbook. It's a fun book that we hope you will find to be informative and enjoyable, testing your knowledge of trivia dealing with world history.

Unlike some other subjects, history is not cut and dried. Thus, although we tried to arrange the chapters so they would encompass certain time frames, this was not always possible. There will be some overlap, even though we tried to hold this to a minimum. Neither could everything in world history be included. How many history books have you seen that are multivolume works? World history is too expansive to be confined to a single book.

You will also notice that not all the chapters in the book are of the same length. Some periods of history just seem to have more interesting or more accessible trivia than do others.

The ground rules are the same as the preceding books in this series. (1) Each chapter's questions are numbered with the corresponding answers listed at the end of that chapter. (2) On multiple-choice questions, the options are always listed either in ascending alphabetical or numeric order. This will help avoid confusion—and unnecessary hints. We're not here to help you with your answers; that would ruin the fun. We will also introduce each chapter with a brief description of the sometimes loose time frame to be covered in that section of the book.

As to the general form of the questions in *Who, What, When, Where, Why in the World of World History:* While the majority of the questions are straightforward with a dash of multiple-choice queries, there will be some "You Match 'em" questions, along with an interesting diversion in the form of "Name Him (or Her)" questions. In the latter, you will be given some facts about a particular historic personality, place, or event. You will then be asked to guess the answer from the information supplied.

And, let's repeat our little warning from the earlier books: Be Careful. Occasionally you will meet up with a trick question or two. Just to keep you on your toes.

Last, but far from least, I want to thank William Streitwieser for going over the manuscript to doublecheck it for historical accuracy. His knowledge of world history was invaluable in combing out those potentially embarrassing errors.

My thanks also to Grace Freedson and Judy Makover of Barron's Educational Series for their support and patience in making this book possible . . . and fun to do.

Finally, I want to thank Richard S. Newcombe of Creators Syndicate for allowing me to use some of the questions that have appeared in my weekly syndicated column, "The Answer Man."

Well, enough of these preliminaries. We hope you enjoy your trip. Let's get started on our journey through *World History*.

Laying the Foundations of Civilization

One of the most-engrossing phases of world history is that period when written languages were first developed. Much is still being uncovered about this era, unveiling new aspects of those "founding" civilizations. While it was a period in which several religions sprang up only to disappear, it also witnessed the birth of many religions that have survived through the scores of centuries that have passed.

While we're looking back at these early centuries, we'll also throw in some questions on the periods leading up to the era of the written word. Let's start out now on our fun- and fact-filled journey through time.

1 A basalt slab, discovered by Napoleon Bonaparte's troops in 1799, led French Egyptologist Jean François Champollion to the key to deciphering Egyptian hieroglyphics. What is the name of this priceless relic, which is now in the British Museum?

2 One of the more interesting early civilizations was that of Mesopotamia. The name means "the country between the rivers." Can you name the famous pair of rivers?

3 Among the first cultures to master the craft of ironworking (700 B.C.–200 A.D.) was an early West African group that had settled near what is now Nigeria. What was the name of this group?

4 King Enmebaragesi is the oldest known historic king (c. 2700 B.C.). Can you name the kingdom over which he ruled?

5 In addition to the process of preserving their dead and installing their departed rulers in elaborate mausoleums, what was unusual about the surroundings provided by the Egyptians for the mummies within the pyramids?

6 For about 200 years (c. 1700–1500 B.C.) Egypt was ruled by an invading Semitic tribe. What was the name of that tribe?

7 The first capital of Egypt was a city whose name is now borne by a well-known U.S. city. What was the name of the first capital of the Land of the Pharaohs?

8 Ironically, it is believed that more is known about some of the pre-Egyptian civilizations than about Egypt itself. This is said to be because of an Egyptian invention. Can you guess what invention deprived us of some historic data?

9 Imhotep was an adviser and physician to the pharaohs, but perhaps his most-noted accomplishment was in another area. Do you know what area this is?

10 What famed Egyptian ruler was Tutankhamen's father-in-law?

11 Among the many fascinating customs of the ancient Egyptians was the process of embalming that resulted in what we know as the mummy. Where did the name *mummy* come from?

12 The Egyptians believed that the god, Khnum, created man. What instrument did they believe Khnum used to accomplish this feat?

13 One of the most important discoveries leading to knowledge of our earliest civilizations was the deciphering of the languages on the Rosetta Stone. Where did the Rosetta Stone get its name?

14 Of what historic importance was the discovery of the laws of Ur-Nammu, king of Ur?

15 Rivers, especially river valleys, have become synonymous with the founding of civilizations, even to be point of their being termed "cradles of civilization." What two rivers—one in Pakistan, the other in China—were the birthplaces of civilization in these two areas?

16 Around 3300 B.C., the earliest form of writing was invented. The process entailed using a reed pressed in soft clay to form wedge-shaped words. What is this type of primitive script called?

17 The oldest regular astronomical observations date back to the first observations of eclipses and novas in the fourteenth century B.C. Where were these observations recorded?

18 The Paleolithic, Mesolithic, and Neolithic periods are divisions of what prehistoric era?

19 Of the periods listed in the preceding question which is considered to be the longest stage in history? (It lasted almost 500,000 years.)

20 Among the earliest tools found in archeological exploration are devices called *fist hatchets*. What is a fist hatchet?

21 In designating the various centuries in time, what do the abbreviations B.C. and A.D. mean in translation?

22 What is the date (year) of the beginnings, respectively, of B.C. and A.D. in the historic calendar?

23 The Bronze Age, that period when metal first came into use, is marked by many historians as the beginning of civilization. Which of the following three important metals did the early humans devise first: bronze, copper, or iron?

24 Four distinct types of humanoids lived during the Lower Paleolithic Age. They were the Heidelberg Man, the Java Man, the Neanderthal, and the Peking Man. We won't ask you to set these in time chronologically. Just tell us which of the four was the most advanced.

25 Potsherds are cited as important to the study of ancient history. What are potsherds?

26 While no method is foolproof, what chemical element is used to attempt to "date" archeological finds?

27 What are megaliths?

28 What is unusual about the directional placement of the Great Pyramid?

29 Here is your first "Name Him" question: He was among the last imperial rulers of ancient Egypt and fathered sixty-seven children. His mummy now rests in the Cairo Museum. Name him.

30 The early Egyptian dynasties divided their regimes into various government districts. What were these districts called?

31 Who was the pharaoh of the First Egyptian Dynasty?

32 Were the early Egyptians monogamous or polygamous?

33 Who was the last king of the Kingdom of Babylon?

34 Recently, archaeologists uncovered the ruins in Egypt of Nekhen, the city that served as the capital of the world's first nation-state. Within 200 years, how long ago was this city the capital of Egypt?

35 Though the phrase has changed over the centuries to encompass peoples of many nations, the word "Semite" originally referred to descendants of Shem. Who was Shem?

36 This custom (unique to India) dates back to at least 600 B.C. What is this social system?

37 The ancient Laws of Hammurabi set a landmark in medicine. What was established by Hammurabi's Laws?

38 What aspect of Hammurabi's Code is referred to as *lex talionis*?

39 Can you name the people who gave us the first civilized community with cuneiform writing, a calendar, and a system of weights and measures?

40 In early Sumeria (c. 2355 B.C.), an enlightened ruler, Uruinimgina, decreed that two segments of the population were to be exempt from taxation by the high priests. What two groups in the Sumerian society were granted tax-exempt status?

41 The ancient Egyptians considered this vegetable a prime source of strength. They reportedly, at one time, spent nine tons of gold to buy a supply of it to feed those engaged in the construction of the pyramids. What was this pyramid-builders' staple?

42 Egyptians of the Sixth Dynasty (c. 2345–2181 B.C.) were firm believers in *ka*. What were *ka*?

43 Although the first examples of eyeglasses for vision improvement are lost in antiquity, the ancients did use a type of magnifying glass. For what purpose did they use them?

44 What type of stone was used to form the (Are you ready for this?) 2.5-ton blocks that went into the construction of King Cheop's Pyramid in Egypt?

45 Which ancient civilization did Hammurabi rule (c. 1792–1750 B.C.)?

46 As with virtually all universal, or multinational, celebrations, New Year's fetes are accompanied by an assortment of unique customs in the various nations. Among the Chinese, the Yang use noise (cymbals and the like) and firecrackers to drive away the Yin. What do the Yang and the Yin represent?

47 Thutmosis III (1504–1450 B.C.) is noted as probably the greatest Egyptian militarist, having undergone twenty years of training in arms. By what nickname is Thutmosis III often called?

48 The travels of Moses have carved a spot for him in history. In what country is it believed Moses was born?

49 You read of Egypt in the pages of the history of Africa, Asia, and Europe. On what continent is Egypt?

50 Before the creation of the famed Hammurabi Code there was the Sumerian Code, which was more moderate. For example, can you cite the difference between the two in their punishment for a woman convicted of adultery?

51 In ancient Babylon, there were some unique rules involved in the marriage of slaves. Can you guess what these unusual rules were?

52 How long (in days) was a year in the Babylonian calendar? And, to make this question even more interesting, how many hours were there in a Babylonian day?

53 It was an Egyptian custom to bury the dead along with a papyrus roll inscribed with prayers and charms to help the departed soul. What is the term used to describe this roll?

54 In 1922 Howard Carter, an archeologist, made a priceless discovery in

Egypt's Valley of the Kings. What was it that Carter uncovered?

55 In a geographic context, what is unique about Upper Egypt and Lower Egypt?

56 Which of the Egyptian pharaohs was the first monotheist?

57 During the Chang Dynasty in China (1766–1122 B.C.) a strange rite was conducted involving the dead. What was this unusual ritual?

58 Although he bore the name Amenhotep IV when he rose to become pharaoh, once he ascended to the throne, the Egyptian ruler changed his name to Akhenaton. Why did he adopt this new name?

59 Ptolemy II (285–246 B.C.) bore the full name Ptolemy II Philadelphus, which was bestowed because of his marriage. What was noteworthy about his marriage to Arsinoe II?

60 The Ptolemies ruled Egypt for almost three centuries. Who was the last of the line to rule the Land of the Pharaohs?

61 The ancient Egyptians did not use yeast to leaven their bread by fermentation. What did they use?

62 Who were the first major sea traders, thus spreading the various cultures and products among many nations?

63 What material was used to wrap Egyptian mummies?

64 Croesus (560–545 B.C.), the last king of the Lydians, was responsible for an innovation that is still in use worldwide every day. What was this unique system?

65 The Greeks had a term for the Semites who occupied the northern coast of Phoenicia (c. 1000 B.C.) that would be quite familiar to today's football fans. What did the Greeks call the Phoenicians?

66 With the death of Solomon (c. 923 B.C.), the Hebrew Kingdom was divided north and south. What were the names, respectively, of each sector?

67 Here's a "Name Him" question for you. He was a Chaldean who ruled for forty-three years. This Oriental monarch destroyed Jerusalem and took many captive Hebrews back to Babylon. Under his rule, the famed Hanging Gardens of Babylon were constructed and great strides were made in astronomy. Name him.

68 A remarkably similar story is told about the infancies of Sargon the Great, ruler of the Akkadians (c. 2340 B.C.), and Moses, the leader of the Israelites some thousand years later. What was similar about the stories of these two leaders' early lives?

69 Hundreds of thousands of cuneiform tablets from the Sumerians (2135–2027 B.C.) have been uncovered over the years. What single subject matter is recorded in the overwhelming majority of these ancient documents?

70 Only one place in the world uses a form of writing that is directly descended from the early Sumerian form. Where is this remnant of that writing style to be found?

71 The first king of Israel met a tragic fate. Who was Israel's first monarch?

72 Between 1000 and 500 B.C. the trade lanes of the Mediterranean Sea were virtually monopolized by the merchant mariners of two nations. What two nations controlled the sea trade during this period in history?

73 What was unusual about the public image adopted by Hatshepsut, who ruled Egypt from 1490 to 1468 B.C.?

74 The Pyramid of Cheops (King Khufu) is one of the Seven Wonders of the World. Within fifty feet guess the height of this architectural marvel. And, for additional credit, guess the number of acres it covers.

75 *Homo erectus*, one of the earliest humanoids, is said to be one of the first of our ancestors to make tools, but what is viewed by many historians as *Homo erectus'* greatest contribution to civilization?

76 Who was the Persian king who conquered Babylon in 539 B.C. and restored the Hebrews' native land, allowing them to rebuild their temple?

77 What was the position in India's caste system of the untouchables?

78 History is rife with mention of the name Cleopatra. But what many readers don't realize is that there was more than one Cleopatra on the throne of Egypt. How many Cleopatras were there on the Egyptian throne? And which of these was the Cleopatra of whom we read so much?

79 The ancients had variant views on the cause of this natural phenomenon. The Japanese blamed a subterranean giant spider, the Mongolians blamed a pig, and in India they said it was a mole. What was the occurrence that stirred these opinions?

80 What factor is believed by historians to have brought about "permanent" communities as opposed to nomadic tribes?

81 We're used to seeing early ships with carved figureheads on their bows, but many of the ancient ships had a decoration still seen occasionally today. It was called *oculi*. What was the oculi? And what purpose did it serve?

82 Hypocausts have been uncovered in ruins both of Roman and Mongol civilizations. What are hypocausts?

83 The word civilization comes from the Greek word *civis*. What does *civis* mean?

84 In 600 B.C. Chinese artisans used an item to glaze their pottery that is used daily in homes today for cleaning purposes. What is this everyday cleaning aid?

85 The oldest known religious document in the world dates back to c. 800 B.C. What document is this?

86 Many of the early "civilizations" engaged in ceremonies that included sacrifices, often using human victims. But what was unusual about the human sacrifices in ancient China?

87 In c. 621 B.C. the chief archon (magistrate) of Athens instituted a code of law that has preserved his name through the ages. Among his sentences was the death penalty for stealing a cabbage. Who was this harsh judge?

Answers

1 *It is the Rosetta Stone, which was inscribed by priests of Ptolemy V in hieroglyphics, demotic (the popular language of Egypt at the time), and with the message repeated on the bottom of the stone in Greek script.*

2 *The rivers were the Tigris and Euphrates. Their Babylonian names were Diklat and Purattu, respectively.*

3 *The early Nigerians were called the Nok culture.*

4 *He was the ruler of Kish, a city in ancient Mesopotamia.*

5 *They were installed in what amounted to apartments with furniture, musical instruments, and even statues of cooks, bakers, and barbers to serve their needs in the afterlife. Later tombs even included bathrooms.*

6 *During this period Egypt was controlled by the Hyksos.*

⑦ *Memphis, Tennessee, was named after Egypt's first capital.*

⑧ *Papyrus, forerunner to our modern paper, caused some of the writings from Egypt to be lost since paper rots with age. The earlier civilizations kept their records on stone tablets for the most part, which have survived the ages.*

⑨ *Imhotep was the pharaoh's architect, and in that capacity he constructed (with a lot of manual help) the first pyramid.*

⑩ *A great military leader, Amenhotep (1398–1353 B.C.), who expanded Egypt's territorial control from the Euphrates to the second cataract of the Nile, was the father of King Tutankhamen's bride, Ankhesnamum.*

⑪ *The process for mummification was to soak the body for weeks in a solution called natron, then to stuff it with pitch before wrapping it. When Arabs discovered the mummies, they thought the black was due to their having been soaked in bitumen, for which the Arabic word is* mumiyah, *or mummy.*

⑫ *The Egyptians believed that Khnum used a potter's wheel to make man.*

⑬ *The name was taken from the city of Rosetta, an important port at the mouth of the Nile River. The city of Rashid now stands on the site of Rosetta.*

⑭ *The laws of Ur-Nammu (c. 2100 B.C.) comprise the earliest preserved lawbook.*

⑮ *The Harappa civilization was born in the Indus River Valley, and in China the first civilization arose near the Huang Ho, or Yellow, River.*

⑯ *It's called cuneiform, from the Latin word,* cuneus, *meaning wedge.*

⑰ *Astronomical observations were made in China during the Shang Dynasty.*

⑱ *They are part of the Stone Age. Paleolithic (Old Stone), Mesolithic (Middle Stone), and Neolithic (New Stone).*

⑲ *The Paleolithic, or Old Stone, Age was history's longest stage, which dates from about 500,000 years ago to 6000 B.C.*

⑳ *Fist hatchets were almond-shaped stones without handles, which could be held easily in one's hand to use for hammering and such.*

㉑ *The abbreviation B.C. means "before Christ," and A.D. means* anno Domini, *or "year of the Lord."*

㉒ *Both periods begin with a Year One. B.C. begins counting back at the year 1 B.C., and A.D. begins with the year 1 A.D. There is no year dated as zero.*

㉓ *Copper was invented first, followed in turn by bronze and, finally, iron.*

㉔ *It was the Neanderthal, who became extinct and was superseded by the Cro-Magnon Man.*

㉕ *Potsherds are broken pottery fragments, which are of exceptional archeological value.*

㉖ *The element is Carbon 14, or radiocarbon, which is in the atmosphere and absorbed by animals, plants, and trees, thus dating them.*

㉗ *Megaliths are huge stone monuments dating from the late Stone Age and early Bronze Age. A good example are those at Stonehenge in Great Britain.*

㉘ *The four sides of the Great Pyramid are oriented according to the four cardinal points—North, South, East, and West, being only a few degrees off.*

㉙ *The prolific imperial ruler of ancient Egypt was Ramses II (c. 1304– c. 1223 B.C.).*

㉚ *The administrative districts of ancient Egypt were called* nomes.

㉛ *The First Dynasty was ruled by Menes in c. 3200 B.C.*

㉜ *It was a mixed society. The majority were monogamous; however, some of the wealthy had several wives.*

㉝ *Nabonidus (556–539 B.C.) was the last Babylonian monarch.*

㉞ *Nekhen (known today by its Greek name, Hierakonpolis) was the capital 5,100 years ago. By the way, its ruler was Narmer, which means catfish.*

㉟ *He was a son of Noah.*

㊱ *It is the custom of social stratification we know as the caste system.*

㊲ *It was the first known code of medical ethics.*

㊳ Lex talionis, *in effect, means the law of retaliation, or, as we've come to know it, "an eye for an eye, and a tooth for a tooth."*

㊴ *It was the Sumerians (c. 3500–2800 B.C.). They inhabited the region near the Persian Gulf.*

㊵ *Orphans and widows.*

④ *The luncheon special was onions. (How would you like to have been around these guys after lunch?)*

④ *Ka were a vital force within each person's body, which preceded their host to face judgment at the seat of Osiris, king of the dead and god of immortality. Those who had erred during their lifetimes were devoured by a monster.*

④ *They were used to concentrate the sun's rays to start fires.*

④ *The construction of the Great Pyramid of Cheops required 2.3-million blocks of limestone.*

④ *Hammurabi was the king of Babylonia.*

④ *The Yin was a force that was female, dark, and passive; the Yang was male, light, and active.*

④ *Thutmosis III is sometimes referred to as the Egyptian Napoleon.*

④ *Although there is no definitive evidence most historians say Moses was born in Egypt.*

④ *Actually, Egypt is on two continents. While most of the nation is in Africa, the Sinai Peninsula, separated from the rest of Egypt by the Suez Canal, is in Asia.*

50 *Under the Sumerian Code, the husband did not even divorce her. He could take a new bride, with the adulteress losing her position as spouse. Under Hammurabi's Code, both the cheating woman and her lover could be put to death.*

51 *Babylonian slaves could marry free women, and the children of their union were free citizens.*

52 *The Babylonian calendar was comprised of twelve months of alternating twenty-nine and thirty days, giving them a 354-day year. Their days were comprised of only twelve hours, but each hour was 120 minutes long.*

53 *The roll is appropriately known as the Book of the Dead.*

54 *It was the tomb of King Tutankhamen, who ruled from 1352 to 1343 B.C. What made the discovery even more valuable was the fact that grave robbers had not found it first as unfortunately was the case in other historic sites.*

55 *Lower Egypt is to the north of Upper Egypt. Thus, when you look at a map, Lower Egypt is at the top, Upper Egypt at the bottom. This is because the Nile River flows north, emptying into the Mediterranean Sea.*

56 *Akhenaton (1379-1362 B.C.), who shunted aside the numerous gods of Egypt* *to worship Aton, was the first pharoah to be a monotheist.*

57 *The dead were burned and their remains were studied in order to read the future by interpreting the cracks in the bones.*

58 *Akhenaton, whose name is often seen spelled several different ways, such as Amenophis, adopted the new name in honor of his newfound god, Aton.*

59 *Philadelphus can be roughly translated into "lover of his sister." The bride, Arsinoe II, was Ptolemy II's sister.*

60 *The last of the Ptolemies to rule was Cleopatra, who committed suicide in 30 B.C.*

61 *The foam from beer was used as a leavening agent by the Egyptian breadmakers.*

62 *The Phoenicians were the first merchant mariners (c. 1000 B.C.).*

63 *Linen. In fact, Tutankhamen's corpse was wrapped in at least sixteen layers of fine linen.*

64 *He introduced coinage.*

65 *Because of their ruddy complexion, the northern Phoenicians were called "redskins" by the Greeks.*

⑥⑥ *The northern kingdom was Israel. The southern was Judah.*

⑥⑦ *The Chaldean ruler was Nebuchadnezzar II (605–562 B.C.).*

⑥⑧ *Both Sargon and Moses were said to have been set adrift on a river in a reed basket by their mothers and adopted by a foster parent.*

⑥⑨ *Some ninety-nine percent of the Sumerian tablets deal with economic matters.*

⑦⓪ *Only Chinese writing can be directly linked to the Sumerian style of text.*

⑦① *Israel's first king was Saul (1030–1010 B.C.), who was killed by the Philistines, along with his three sons, in the Battle of Mount Gilboa.*

⑦② *Phoenician and Greek vessels dominated the Mediterranean trade in that period.*

⑦③ *Hatshepsut had herself represented to the people of Egypt as a man. She also claimed to be a descendent of the god Amon.*

⑦④ *The Pyramid is 500-plus feet high and covers some 13-plus acres.*

⑦⑤ Homo erectus *was the first to tame and use fire.*

⑯ *Cyrus.*

⑰ *The untouchables were the undesirables. They were beneath and outside of the castes, only because of their being born into the untouchable strata.*

⑱ *There were seven Cleopatras. The one linked with Marc Antony and Julius Caesar was Cleopatra VII (69–30 B.C.)*

⑲ *These were the objects each believed caused earthquakes.*

⑳ *Agriculture made it possible, and even necessary, for early civilizations to plant communal, as well as horticultural, roots.*

㉑ Oculi *are carved or painted eyes on the ship's bow to guide the craft clear of danger.*

㉒ *Hypocausts are floor heating units, wherein the floor rests on piles of bricks in the foundation, leaving spaces between them. Fires are kept burning beneath the floors, thus heating them.*

㉓ Civis *means city.*

㉔ *The Chinese artisans used borax to glaze their pottery.*

㉕ *It's the* Rig-Veda *of India. In translation,* Rig *means hymn, and* Veda *means knowledge.*

86 *In ancient China, human sacrifices were not limited to single victims. In fact, human sacrifices sometimes took the lives of 100 or more people in a single ceremony.*

87 *If you thought his penalty in the cabbage theft was draconian, you came up with his name. The chief archon was Draco, from whose name the word* draconian *evolved.*

Wrestling with the Greco-Roman Dominance

The decline of the Egyptian domination of history was followed by the rise of the Greek and later the Roman empires.

This was one of history's more fascinating periods, providing fuel for later literary and artistic masterpieces.

While there is much emphasis on the Greek and Roman influence in this chapter, it was a period in which the Eastern cultures were also taking form. Therefore, we have included some questions regarding these groups, as well as the birth of Christianity, which has had immeasurable impact on the ensuing eras. So let us begin our quiz on these fascinating societies.

❶ Among this Greek mathematician's contributions to following centuries were the ratio of pi (3.1416), the invention of pulleys and levers, and the use of a screw within a cylinder to raise water. Who was this genius who lived from 287 to 212 B.C.?

❷ Arguably the most famous book to come out of ancient India (around the fourth century) is a rather explicit sex manual that has often been banned. The author claimed it was a religious look at sex. Can you name this book?

❸ Of what import to historians are the "Bamboo Annals"?

❹ The *Pax Romana* (30 B.C.–170 A.D.) was noteworthy for the relative peace, expanded commerce, speedy travel on the Roman highways, and the extension of relatively even-handed justice, even to captured peoples. Under what emperor did the *Pax Romana* come into fruition?

❺ For various reasons, the spoken dialects in different regions of China were often incomprehensible to people from other regions. How then could they communicate with one another?

6 What are the Dead Sea Scrolls? And, for extra credit, where were they discovered?

7 In early Rome there were two main social classes, the wealthy landowners and the class comprising all other freemen (peasants, merchants, and artisans). What are these two classes called?

8 The Mauryan Empire (321–184 B.C.) was the first in India's history to unite all of Hindustan and helped spread Buddhism throughout Southeast Asia. While the empire's name is derived from that of Chandragupta Maurya, it reached its peak under the emperor who followed Maurya. Who was this emperor?

9 Name the first pope.

10 Jesus was born in Bethlehem, but his parents, Joseph and Mary, were from Nazareth in Galilee. With her expecting a child, why did they travel to Bethlehem in Judea?

11 Siddharta Gautama was born in India in 563 B.C., a member of the second caste, which made him a warrior. By what name do we know Gautama?

12 We currently use the Gregorian calendar, which corrected computational errors in its predecessor—the Julian calendar. For whom were the two calendars named, respectively?

13 The original Saint Nicholas lived in Myra in the fourth century. Myra is now what country?

14 The ancient Roman Feast of Lupercalia included a lottery. What was raffled off during this celebration?

15 What Roman emperor issued the Edict of Milan (313 A.D.), which granted religious toleration to Christians?

16 The ancient Greeks had a game similar to our modern football. What did they use as a ball?

17 This popular board game is believed to date back some 1,400 years to either Persia or India. Can you name it?

18 Under what oppressive dynasty was China's first strong central government formed?

19 The founder of Buddhism is believed to have conquered *Karma* and achieved *Nirvana*. What are Karma and Nirvana?

20 In 108 B.C. the forces of Emperor Wu Ti of the Han Dynasty conquered Choson. By what name do we know Choson?

21 A famed adage on being above reproach is: "Caesar's wife should be above suspicion." To whom is this attributed?

22 We are affected everyday by the decimal point, the zero, and Arabic numerals, and so we take these basics for granted. But in what society did they originate?

23 The Jewish celebration Hanukkah is known as the Festival of Lights. What does this commemorate?

24 Time for a "Who Said It?" question. "There is only one good, knowledge, and one evil, ignorance." Who Said It: (a) Horace, (b) Plato, (c) Socrates, or (d) Virgil?

25 The name of the Feast of Lupercalia was changed by Pope Gelasius in 494 A.D. What was the new name?

26 This being a book of world history trivia, it's only appropriate that we ask: Who is most often recognized as the first great historian?

27 Unlike the carvings in caves linked to prehistoric humans, the caves in the Ajanta Hills of India tell a different story for historians. Who created the Ajanta artwork? And, how do these caves differ from the earlier ones?

28 Throughout the centuries gold has been rated as the sign of wealth, but in ancient China an item made by humans was worth more than its weight in gold. What was this priceless commodity?

29 Along with the Yin and Yang, the Chinese explained the universe in terms of the Five Elements. Care to venture a guess as to what these five were?

30 The Olympics of 520 B.C. included foot races that would have been well worth watching. What was so unusual about these matches?

31 Yet another event of the ancient games was the pankration. What was the pankration?

32 What was London called when it was originally founded in the first century?

33 What people founded the site that would one day become London?

34 What is the meaning of a Roman numeral with a bar above it?

35 At the time of the Nativity, Bethlehem was ruled by Herod the Great, who had been appointed king of Judaea by the Romans. What connection was there between this despot and Marc Antony?

36 In ancient days one of the most-feared and most-disliked public figures was the publican. What was a publican?

37 Cited both in history and in tales of fiction is a famed mountain pass on the border separating Afghanistan and Pakistan. Can you name this famous passageway that Alexander the Great used in his conquests?

38 Few men in history have conquered as much territory as did Alexander the Great. How old was Alexander III when he died?

39 Here's a "Name Him" question. He was perhaps the most mentally incompetent and cruel of Rome's emperors, who once reputedly named a horse to the senate in order to humiliate the senators. His real name was Gaius Caesar, but he is better known by a nickname, which means "little boots." Name him.

40 Who was the emperor of the Roman Empire at the time of Jesus' birth?

41 K'ung Fu-tse (c. 551–479 B.C.) preached the five virtues: humanity, courtesy, honesty, moral wisdom, and steadfastness. By what name do we know K'ung Fu-tse?

42 What does Buddha mean?

43 By what name do we know Saul of Tarsus?

44 One of the most important items to a young Roman in ancient days was a bulla. What was a bulla?

45 Many historians question the story of Emperor Nero playing the fiddle while Rome burned in the year 64 A.D. Others say that, if the story is true, he would not have been playing a fiddle, but another instrument. Can you name the instrument?

46 The ancient Roman Parentalia has been described as being much like our modern Father's Day. Aside from the fact that the Parentalia lasted ten days, can you guess the major difference between the two observances?

47 Athens reached its apex both in power and prosperity between 461 and 429 B.C. Who was the ruler of Athens during this peak period?

48 The world's first encyclopedia was produced in c. 23–79 A.D. What was the work's title, and who produced it?

49 One of the most famous assassinations in history is that of Julius Caesar. In his will, Caesar bequeathed his money and power to his grandnephew Octavius (sometimes called Octavian). By what name do we know this heir to Julius Caesar?

50 Here's a two-part question for you. (a) Name the Seven Wonders of the World, and (b) tell how many of them still exist.

51 The polis was of great importance in ancient Greece. What was a polis?

52 You may not be able to cite the accomplishments of Philip II Amyntas, but if you've studied your history you are aware of those of his son. Who was Philip's famous son?

53 We hear reference to the *Decalogue* fairly often. By what name do we know the *Decalogue*?

54 Who was Alexander the Great's immortal tutor?

55 Where did we get the word *alphabet* to describe our written characters?

56 The Great Wall of China was constructed during the reign of Ch'in Shih-Huang Ti (221–206 B.C.) to defend against foreign invaders. Who were these invaders?

57 The Greek city of Peritas was named by Alexander the Great in honor of a friend. Who was this friend of whom the conqueror thought so highly?

58 The epic poems the *Iliad* and the *Odyssey* deal with events in a particular war. Against whom was the war waged?

59 The enmity between Carthage and Rome in the three Punic Wars was underlined by such statements as that frequently espoused in speeches by Marcus Cato. The senator closed most of his speeches with the statement, "Carthago delendo est" (Carthage must be destroyed). What did the Romans do to "destroy" Carthage when they finally captured the city in 146 B.C.?

60 Ancient Athenians had the power to vote to banish any citizen they thought was a danger to the community. The ballot on which the name of the accused was written was a piece of pottery called an *ostrakon*. What modern word evolved from this practice?

61 The main city-states of ancient Greece were Athens and Sparta. One was a democratic society, steeped in education and the arts. The other was an aristocracy, based on militarism. Which was which?

62 Name the two chief protagonists in the Peloponnesian War (431–404 B.C.).

63 Here's a "Name Him" question. This famed ancient Greek bard, who is believed to have written the *Iliad* and the *Odyssey*, was also famous as a religious instructor. Name him.

64 The alphabet upon which all others in the Western World evolved was first put to use in ancient Greece. Where did the Greeks get this early alphabet?

65 It was in the Second Punic War that Hannibal carved his name deeply into history by crossing a mountain range with his infantry, cavalry, and elephants. What mountain range did Hannibal's troops cross?

66 Hannibal's defeat of the Romans at Cannae in 216 B.C. made military history. Why?

67 Egypt's Queen Cleopatra has often been the subject of romantic literary works. The Nile queen was married three times. What made Cleopatra's first two marriages extremely unusual (and virtually unheard of today)?

68 Speaking of the famed Queen of the Nile, one of William Shakespeare's many immortal plays is *Antony and Cleopatra*, which is based on the multinational love affair. How did these ill-starred lovers die?

69 When one speaks of philosophy, the immortal Greek trio, Aristotle, Plato, and Socrates, must be mentioned. One of these three set the pace, and in turn was followed by another, who became the mentor for the last of them. Your chore is to set these philosophers in chronological order.

70 You have probably learned of Socrates' dramatic suicide by taking hemlock. But, what provoked the Greek philosopher to take his own life?

71 Greek architecture is still much used and much admired. Name the three styles of Greek architecture.

72 Philip II of Macedonia (382–336 B.C.) conquered all of the Greek city-states, except one. Which of the city-states did not fall to Philip?

73 How old was Alexander the Great when Philip of Macedon died and Alexander took command?

74 Early art did not include a human image of the god Buddha. What event changed this?

75 Not much is known about the early days of the city of Rome. Why is this?

76 Until the invaders were overthrown (c. 500 B.C.), the Romans were oppressively ruled by people who had migrated from Asia Minor and settled north of Rome. Who were these immigrants?

77 To keep the peasants occupied, Roman politicians presented them with such diversions as the contests of gladiators and chariot races. What was the name (which is still used in the field of entertainment) for the race courses used for chariot races?

78 Here's an easy question for you: On what date was Julius Caesar assassinated? (Real history buffs must include the year.)

79 Who was the first man to serve as emperor of the Roman Empire?

80 What do the cities of Byzantium, Constantinople, and Istanbul have in common?

81 Where did the term *Caesarean section*, in reference to a baby being delivered by cutting through the walls of the abdomen, originate?

82 This Chinese invention, dating back to 105 A.D., according to some estimates, was kept under wraps until Arabs captured one of those who knew the secret manufacturing process. What was this top-secret invention?

83 Name the man who fathered modern medicine in the fifth century B.C.

84 Pompeii, as in "The Last Days of . . . ," is most famous for the fact that it was buried by a volcanic eruption that killed thousands. Name the volcano that wreaked havoc on the Italian village in 79 A.D.

85 In discussions of the modern Olympics there's much ado about the number of medals won by the various nations' athletes. But there were no medals awarded at the first recorded Olympics in 776 B.C. What was the symbol of excellence for those Games?

86 To whose honor were the first Olympic Games dedicated?

87 A religion founded in Persia in the sixth century B.C. is still practiced by descendants of those who fled to India in the eighth century A.D. to escape Muslim persecution. Can you name the founder of this religion?

88 The modern marathon received its name as a result of Athens' 490 B.C.

upset victory on the Plain of Marathon in Greece over a superior Persian force led by Darius I. How is this battle linked to racing?

89 Here's a "Who Said It?" question. "Do not count your chickens before they hatch." Who said it: (a) Aesop, (b) Aristotle, (c) Homer, or (d) Lao Tzu?

Answers

① *Archimedes.*

② *Vatsyayana, author of the* Kamasutra, *described his work as "in perfect accordance with the Holy Scriptures."*

③ *"The Bamboo Annals," which were found in a grave in 281 A.D., are an early history of China written on bamboo slips, which were used as paper in early China.*

④ *The* Pax Romana *began under the emperor Caesar Augustus and lasted into the reign of Marcus Aurelius.*

⑤ *Although they had different dialects, the written text (characters) was virtually the same.*

⑥ *The Scrolls were the library of a Jewish sect of the first century A.D. They contain, among other writings, almost the entire Old*

Testament. They were discovered in caves in the Negev Desert near the Dead Sea in 1947.

⑦ *The wealthy were called the patricians, and the freemen were called the plebeians.*

⑧ *The principal ruler during the Mauryan Empire was the Emperor Asoka.*

⑨ *Saint Peter the apostle.*

⑩ *They were going to be counted in a census for tax purposes. Bethlehem was the city of David from whom Joseph descended. And the emperor's edict said the citizens had to return to the city of their ancestors.*

⑪ *Gautama, after witnessing the misery surrounding him, formed his own religion, Buddhism, the designation of which is taken from his adopted name, Buddha.*

⑫ *The Gregorian was named for Pope Gregory XIII. And the Julian for Gaius Julius Caesar.*

⑬ *Turkey.*

⑭ *Young men drew the names from a pot of young maidens who would then be their courting partners for the coming year. Christians changed this to drawing the names of a saint, whose virtues were to be emulated by the person who drew the saint's name.*

(15) *The Edict of Milan was issued by Constantine the Great (c. 288–337), who reportedly was baptized on his deathbed.*

(16) *The "ball" was an inflated cow's bladder.*

(17) *The game is chess.*

(18) *It was under the Ch'in Dynasty (221–206 B.C.), from which, by the way, the name China is derived. The ruler called himself Ch'in Shih (first) Huang (emperor) Ti (deity of the Shang Dynasty).*

(19) *Karma is fate or destiny, and Nirvana is release from the necessity of rebirth after death.*

(20) *Korea.*

(21) *Julius Caesar himself is so-quoted in* Plutarch's Lives.

(22) *All originated during the Gupta Empire in India under Chandragupta II, who died in 415 A.D.*

(23) *Hanukkah marks the anniversary of the rededication by the Maccabees in 165 B.C. of the Temple in Jerusalem.*

㉔ *(c) Socrates (469–399 B.C.) wrote this in* Diogenes Laertius.

㉕ *Pope Gelasius renamed the celebration Saint Valentine's Day.*

㉖ *The first great historian was Herodotus (c. 484–424 B.C.).*

㉗ *Ajanta's cave art was created by early Buddhist monks between 200 B.C. and 700 A.D. The caves were used as temples. The art illustrates events in the life of Buddha.*

㉘ *The priceless commodity was silk, which was woven in China more than 4,000 years ago. For many centuries silk was the chief item in China's foreign trade.*

㉙ *They were wood, fire, earth, metal, and water.*

㉚ *The participants in the 520 B.C. games were soldiers in full armor, although it should be noted the armor was not of the bulky, full-body form of the medieval period.*

㉛ *The pankration—"The Game of All Powers"—(648 B.C.) was a man-to-man battle using any method possible to win, boxing, wrestling, kicking, biting, choking, eye-gouging, and, yes, there were fatalities.*

㉜ *London was settled in the first century as Londinium.*

(33) *The Romans founded Londinium. They left in the fifth century.*

(34) *It means the numeral should be multiplied by 1,000. For example: The letter V is the Roman numeral for five. But place a bar over it, and it becomes 5,000.*

(35) *It was Marc Antony, a friend of Herod, who managed to get him the appointment as king of Judaea.*

(36) *A publican was a tax collector. (Just shows you things don't change much over time.)*

(37) *It's the Khyber Pass.*

(38) *Alexander the Great was only thirty-three years old when he died in 323 B.C.*

(39) *We call this emperor Caligula. He reigned from 37 to 41 A.D.*

(40) *Caesar Augustus was the emperor of Rome at the time of the birth of Christianity.*

(41) *We know K'ung Fu-tse by the name of Confucius.*

(42) *"The Enlightened One."*

(43) *Saint Paul; Saul took the name Paul upon becoming a Christian.*

⑭ *It was a leather or metal case containing amulets, which was placed around the child's neck by the father soon after birth— a good luck charm. The girls wore theirs until they were married; the boys until they donned the toga of manhood.*

⑮ *Some say Nero would have been playing a lyre, which is a harp-like instrument.*

⑯ *The Parentalia was not for living fathers. Ovid is quoted as saying the observance was to "appease the souls of your fathers."*

⑰ *The Athenian general who ruled in this period was Pericles (495–429 B.C.).*

⑱ *It was the thirty-seven-volume* Natural History *(or* Historia Naturalis*) of Pliny the Elder.*

⑲ *Octavius became the Emperor Augustus Caesar.*

⑳ *The Seven Wonders are (a) The Egyptian Pyramids at Giza, the Hanging Gardens of Babylon, the Statue of Zeus (Jupiter) at Olympia, the Colossus of Rhodes, the Mausoleum of Halicarnassus, the Lighthouse of Pharos (Alexandria), and the Temple of Diana (Artemis) at Ephesus. (b) Only the Pyramids remain.*

(51) *The polis was a city-state. In effect, the city was a state in and of itself.*

(52) *If "The Answer Man" had told you that Philip was better known as Philip of Macedon you might have more easily answered that he was the father of the world-conquering Alexander the Great.*

(53) *The Ten Commandments.*

(54) *Aristotle.*

(55) *The word* alphabet *comes from the first two letters in the Greek alphabet, alpha and beta.*

(56) *The 1,500-mile-long Great Wall was constructed to protect China against the Hsiung-nu, or Huns, from the north.*

(57) *It was his dog. (Most dog lovers can well understand this.)*

(58) *The* Iliad *told of the Greek expedition against Troy. The* Odyssey *told of Odysseus' adventures while returning from that encounter.*

(59) *The Romans burned Carthage, plowed under its ruins, and salted the furrows to ensure that the soil would no longer be fertile.*

(60) *The word* ostracize *comes from the name for the piece of pottery, the ostrakon.*

(61) *Athens was the democratic society. Sparta was based on military training.*

(62) *Sparta and Athens clashed in the Peloponnesian War with Sparta coming out on top.*

(63) *Homer (c. 700 B.C.).*

(64) *It was based on the twenty-two-letter alphabet brought to Greece by Phoenician traders.*

(65) *The Alps.*

(66) *The Carthaginian general's forces killed 45,000 Romans* in one afternoon, *which was more casualties in one day than the British Royal Air Force lost in both World War I and II combined.*

(67) *Cleopatra's first husband was her brother, Ptolemy XII, and, following his death, she married her other brother, Ptolemy XIII. This was the custom in ancient Egypt. Her last husband was the Roman, Marc Antony. Adding to the literary intrigue of Cleopatra's love life is the fact that she was also Julius Caesar's mistress.*

68 *Both committed suicide. Mark Antony is said to have fallen on his sword, and it is believed that Cleopatra did indeed let an asp bite her. The poisonous serpent was the symbol of divine royalty in ancient Egypt.*

69 *Coincidentally, these early geniuses went in reverse alphabetical order. Socrates (496–399 B.C.) was the role model for his follower, Plato (c. 427–348 B.C.). And Aristotle (384–322 B.C.), then, studied under Plato.*

70 *An Athenian court, finding Socrates guilty of corrupting the minds of his students with his impious preaching, had sentenced him to death.*

71 *The three styles of Greek architecture are Doric, Ionic, and Corinthian.*

72 *Sparta was the lone holdout against Philip's army.*

73 *Alexander was twenty years old when his father died.*

74 *The invasion of India by Alexander the Great brought with it the influence of Greco-Roman sculptors leading to reproductions of Buddha in human form.*

75 *The founding days of Rome are lost in antiquity because the early Italians had no written language.*

(76) The Etruscans ruled Rome from their invasion in 750 until 500 B.C.

(77) The chariot race courses were called circuses, which over the years became shows rather than contests.

(78) If you've read your Shakespeare, you'd know it as the Ides of March, or March 15, 44 B.C.

(79) Caesar Augustus (63 B.C.–14 A.D.) was the first emperor of Rome.

(80) They are all the same city. Byzantium was the ancient Greek name of the city on the Bosporus. The Emperor Constantine (324–337 A.D.) renamed it in his own honor in 330 A.D. And in 1930 the Turkish government renamed it Istanbul.

(81) It is believed that Julius Caesar was born in this manner.

(82) It was paper, which was made from decaying vegetable matter. (Some critics now claim that certain books still retain an odor of decaying matter.)

(83) It was Hippocrates of Cos, best remembered for the Hippocratic Oath.

(84) Mount Vesuvius.

⑧⑤ *The victors in the 776 B.C. Olympics were rewarded with wild olive crowns, signifying peace.*

⑧⑥ *The 776 B.C. games were held in honor of Apollo, the Greek god.*

⑧⑦ *The Parsees, descendants of those who fled from Persia, practice Zoroastrianism, which is based on the teachings of Zoroaster, who lived in the sixth century B.C.*

⑧⑧ *The Athenian leader in the battle, Miltiades, dispatched Pheidippides to carry the news of the Greek victory to Athens. Pheidippides ran the distance, delivered the message, then collapsed and died. The marathon race is in his honor.*

⑧⑨ *(a) Aesop (c. 550 B.C.) said it in* The Milkmaid and Her Pail.

The Path to—
and from—
the Middle Ages

I'M SORRY, SIR RUFUS, BUT A CAN OPENER IS A DEFINITE NO-NO IN A JOUST.

The period we call the Middle Ages (roughly from 500 to 1500 A.D.) has come down through history as one of the most romanticized eras. It was also a time in which religion, with the rise of the Islamic and Christian influence, had far more control over daily events than is the case today.

Although we tend to forget that we would have to give up many of our modern conveniences if we were to venture back to medieval times, it's fun to dream of meeting the likes of King Arthur and Robin Hood.

So take up your armor, don your helmet, grab your sword and lance, and let's *wander back a few centuries. We'll take you into the age of knights and maidens with side trips for a look at some of the other cultures of that period of history.*

① What event occurred in 476 that is most often used to mark the beginning of the Middle Ages?

② In the British monarchy, there were three Richards—I, II, and III. Which of them was known as Richard Coeur de Lion, or Richard, the Lion-Heart?

③ The Doomsday (or Domesday) Book was created in England in 1086 A.D., during the reign of William the Conqueror. What was listed in this work?

④ This building, one of the most famous in the world, is sometimes called the "Temple of Reason." By what name do we know this structure, which dates back to 1163?

⑤ When a witch is depicted in flight she is usually shown riding a broomstick. According to experts on witchcraft, this is not the method of flight our ancestors depicted as being used by witches. What implements were most often used to describe airborne witches in the Middle Ages?

6 Nicholas Breakspear caused a stir in 1155 by granting Henry II the sovereignty over Ireland. What empowered Breakspear to make this grant?

7 The turbaned Sikhs of India have many customs alien to Westerners, but one in particular has to do with the male Sikhs' names. What is it?

8 We've all grown up remembering the sight of Nativity scenes, especially around Christmas time. Who is considered to have been the one who originated the creche display?

9 The *Angevins* played an important role in British history. Who were they?

10 Who was the author of the twenty-two-volume *Summa Theologica*, an encyclopedia of theology?

11 Ghana, possibly the first kingdom founded in West Africa, reached its peak in the ninth and tenth centuries. By controlling the trade of two natural resources, one to its north, the other to its south, Ghana was able to reach its apex. What were these two important elements?

12 You may not know him by his original name—Giovanni di Bernardone—but he founded one of the most famous religious orders of the Catholic Church. Who was this famed church leader?

13 The invention of gunpowder in China during the eighth century was, as is often the case, an accident. The Chinese alchemists were seeking a completely different product. What were they attempting to produce?

14 When Muslims pray they always face the shrine of Islam in the Great Mosque in Mecca. Of what significance is Mecca, and what is the name of the sacred shrine to which they kneel in honor?

15 Here's a "Match 'em" question. In the first column "The Answer Man" is going to give you the name of a geographic area. See if you can match it with the invaders who were in control of it at the close of the fifth century. Remember this does not mean they retained control, just that they had control at that time in history.

Land Area	Conquerors
1. Britain	**(a)** Anglo-Saxons
2. Italy	**(b)** Ostrogoths
3. North Africa	**(c)** Vandals
4. Spain	**(d)** Visigoths

16 In the fifth century King Alaric led the Visigoths in the conquest of Rome. When Alaric died in 410 his troops provided a highly unusual burial site. What was the burial plot arranged for Alaric by the Visigoths?

17 The first paper money came into use in the eleventh century. In what country was this form of money first instituted?

18 In 1325 the Aztecs, who had been mercenaries and vassals during their existence in the Valley of Mexico, finally settled at Tenochtitlán. What does *Tenochtitlán* mean in translation?

19 We hear much of the seven deadly sins, which the ancients believed would lead to damnation. Can you name these damnable offenses?

20 The word "assassin" has an interesting origin. From what language did the word evolve? And what was its original meaning?

21 Who was the founder of the Muslim faith?

22 The founding of the Muslim faith, Islam, is dated from the *hegira*. What is the hegira?

㉓ The *Koran*, a collection of Mohammed's sayings, authorizes polygamy, but it did set a limit on the number of wives. What was that limit?

㉔ The *Koran* also established the rule requiring the practice of *purdah*, which is still around today in the Middle East. What is purdah?

㉕ Can you name the two branches of Islam?

㉖ One of the literary works which some historians say reveals much of life in early Baghdad is a work we know as the *Arabian Nights*, or *The Thousand and One Nights*. Can you name the storyteller in this book?

㉗ In 1187 a Turkish leader, who had already conquered Egypt, captured Jerusalem. This coup resulted in the Third Crusade, which is the most famous of the series of Crusades. Can you name this Turkish warlord?

㉘ Spain was under the control of Muslims until a marriage in 1469 united the Christian opposition. Name the two monarchs whose wedding marked the downfall of the Muslims in Spain.

㉙ By 1517 the Ottoman Turks had conquered Syria and Egypt. Where did the Ottoman Turks originate?

30 Due to its isolation, England was not deeply involved in early European history. But in the sixth and seventh centuries, the Angles and the Saxons invaded the island. From where in Europe did the Angles and Saxons emigrate?

31 In what year did William the Conqueror lead the Norman invasion of England?

32 We're all familiar with the Norse word *Valhalla*. Is this the Norse equivalent of Heaven where anyone who dies without sin may enter?

33 Were the serfs in the Middle Ages slaves?

34 The Crusades were a series of attempts to wrest control of the Holy Land from the Muslims. How many Crusades were launched?

35 Whether there was in fact a real King Arthur is still disputed among historians. Can you name the Welsh cleric who gave the most impetus to the Arthurian legend with his *Historia Regum Britanniae (History of the Kings of Britain)* in 1136?

36 Arthur's sword, which he reputedly extracted from the stone, a feat no one else could accomplish, is one of the few weapons people can identify by name. What was the name of Arthur's sword?

37 In what country did knights first come into being?

38 In the fourteenth century, England became the first nation in history to establish an effective bicameral parliament. What is a *bicameral* parliament?

39 Who were the original Vikings?

40 In France, they were called *trouveres*. In Germany, they were the *minnesingers*. By what name would we know these special knights?

41 What were the two apprentice stages a youth went through on his way to knighthood?

42 The assault on early castles, especially those constructed of wood, often included the use of *Greek fire*. What was Greek fire?

43 Many literary classics have been based on the life and murder of Thomas à Becket by four of King Henry II's men. What key position did Becket hold at the time of his death?

44 You don't hear an awful lot in history studies about the Battle of Crecy.

But this French-British confrontation in the Hundred Years' War had a good deal of impact on future conflicts. What was initiated in this August 26, 1346, encounter?

45 Early in the fifth century, a Germanic tribe, the Vandals, was well-rooted in Spain until the tribe was unseated by the Goths, another tribe. The Vandals fled across the Strait of Gibraltar, which brings us to our question: How wide is the famed Strait of Gibraltar *at its narrowest point*?

46 The Germanic tribes known as the Goths were called Ostrogoths and Visigoths. What did the prefixes designate?

47 Roman Law, a model for European legal systems for centuries, was codified in the *Corpus Juris Civilis* in 535. By what name is this codification known?

48 The death toll estimates of the number of Europeans wiped out in the Black Plague in the 1300s range from one quarter to three quarters of the population. What disease decimated the Europeans in the Black Plague?

49 How was the infectious disease that brought about the Black Plague spread to humans?

50 Name the man who first declared that the title of pope was to be reserved for the bishop of Rome.

51 Here's a "Who Said It?" question. "In this sign shalt thou conquer." Who Said It: (a) Saint Thomas Aquinas, (b) Chang Heng, (c) Constantine, or (d) Dante Alighieri?

52 Kublai Khan, the first emperor of China's Yuan dynasty, unveiled a new weapon in battles against the Japanese in 1274 and 1281. What was this innovative weapon?

53 Joan of Arc (c. 1412–31) was important to the victory of France over England in the Hundred Years' War, but was captured and burned at the stake. What were the charges that brought the death penalty? And by whom was she tried and convicted?

54 Although Joan of Arc was from Domremy in Lorraine she is known as the Maid of Orleans. Where did that nickname originate?

55 The early monks did a great service to the literary world. Can you cite it?

56 The world's first newspaper appeared in the year 748 A.D. Where was it printed?

57 What major effect did the introduction of the Confucian philosophy have on ancient Japan?

58 No one knows definitively where St. Patrick was born (many believe he was in fact a Scot), but it is known that he was not born in Ireland. Under what circumstances did he travel to Ireland?

59 Britain's Magna Carta, which declared that even a king should be subject to the rule of law, was a forerunner to the U.S. Constitution. In what year did King John place his seal on the Magna Carta?

60 The mayor of Pisa, Italy, closed the famed Leaning Tower to tourists in 1990 because of danger that it might topple. Can you guess (or do you know) the age and the height of the Leaning Tower of Pisa?

61 In the Battle of Agincourt (October 24, 1415), British forces, though outnumbered almost four to one by French knights, won the day. What weapon and tactic in this battle in the Hundred Years' War wrought the upset, changing the feudal form of warfare?

62 Islam is the Arabic name for Mohammed's religion. What does *Islam* mean?

63 Naturally, Mosques (Muslim churches) differ from Christian churches in their decor. But certain types of decorations found in Christian churches are specifically forbidden in mosques. Can you name these? (This does not mean obvious items of Christian worship, such as crosses.)

64 His name was Carolus Magnus, or Charles the Great. But, by what name does history know him?

65 When we receive an *accolade* it usually means some reward as a sign of respect, but what was an accolade in the Medieval Age?

66 A foul often referred to today in boxing matches was also applicable in the Middle Ages in jousting matches between knights. What is the common expression?

67 Albion was the original name of which European country? (Hint: The word Albion comes from the Latin *albus*, meaning white.)

68 In Geoffrey Chaucer's classic *The Canterbury Tales*, which were written in the late fourteenth century, the tales are being told by a group on their way to visit a tomb in the cathedral at Canterbury. Whose tomb were they journeying to visit?

69 We're all familiar with the story of Lady Godiva's horseback ride through her village naked. But do you know: (a) why she took the ride, and (b) the name of the village in which it took place?

70 Can you give the main difference between the guilds of the Middle Ages and our present-day labor unions?

71 King John of Bohemia was killed in the Battle of Crecy (1346). What personal trait marked John as especially gallant?

72 At the Council of Clermont (1095) Pope Urban II issued a proclamation that would have a deep effect on history for the next two centuries. What was precipitated by Pope Urban's proclamation?

73 What are the respective titles of a man and a woman who are knighted?

74 Probably the most tragic of the Crusades occurred in the year 1212. It bore no number, but fell between the Fourth Crusade and the Fifth. Can you explain this unusual Crusade?

75 The legend of Robin Hood builds around the capture and imprisonment of Richard I on his return from the Third Crusade. Who held Richard in custody following his capture?

76 When we hear the pope mentioned, we automatically think of the leader of the Roman Catholic Church, but originally all bishops and priests bore the title. What does the word *pope* mean?

77 The code of conduct linked to the Samurai warriors of Japan dates to the Kamakura shogunate of the twelfth century. It demands total loyalty to the emperor and didn't end until the close of World War II. What is the name of this fierce loyalty?

78 During India's first Muslim empire, the Delhi Sultanate (1192–1398), established by Aybeh, a general, was labeled the "slave dynasty." Why was it so called?

79 In the seventh century A.D., the Byzantines used a secret weapon in naval combat against Arab fleets. What was this weapon?

80 Two knightly orders were created during the Crusades. One was charged with caring for the sick and wounded. The other was established for the protection of pilgrims. Can you name the two orders of knights?

81 The *Great Encyclopedia* of the Emperor Yung Lo made its appearance in 1408. How many volumes comprised the *Great Encyclopedia*, and how many copies were produced?

82 When Jerusalem fell during the First Crusade (1099), the Crusader chosen to be the first Crusader ruler of Jerusalem refused the title of king. He was instead titled Defender (or Protector) of the Holy Sepulchre. Who was the *Defender of the Holy Sepulchre*?

83 You've probably seen pictures of the yeoman warders in current-day England who are garbed in ancient uniforms when guarding the Tower of London. These warders carry a weapon dating to the thirteenth century. It's a combination battle-axe and spear. What is this ancient weapon called?

84 The word *gazette* in reference to newspapers dates back to the *gazettas* of Venice in the Middle Ages. Venetian "newspapers" were announcements posted on walls. They derived their name from a Venetian coin, called the gazetta. Why were these posted newspapers named after a coin?

85 For many years Marco Polo served the Tartar emperor at his court in what is now China. Name the famed emperor.

86 It is believed that, along with all the spices, gems, silks, and the like, brought back to Europe by early traders (most notably, Marco Polo) was a food that has become one of the most popular dishes in the world. What was this product, which the ancient Chinese made from rice and bean flour?

87 A popular TV series relative to early Japan was based on the book by James Clavell titled *Shogun*. Where did the term, *shogun*, originate?

88 Because of its isolation as an island, not much is known about the ancient history of Japan. But it is known that among its earliest inhabitants were the Ainu. What was unique about the Ainu?

89 Here's a two-part question for you. (a) What was the Hanseatic League, and (b) where did it get its name?

90 With the fall of Constantinople in 1453 came the end of an empire that dated back to 330 A.D. What was this empire, and who were the invaders that closed its chapter in world history?

91 In reading about the various monarchs, we often come across the word *regent* or *regency*. What does this designate?

92 In the early thirteenth century, the Tartars invaded Russia from the Far East, but their bid for conquest was halted, albeit temporarily, by the death of their famed leader in 1227. Name this famed Tartar leader.

93 What was the purpose of the Spanish Inquisition?

94 Who was the original and most famous of the *Grand Inquisitors*?

95 Where did the Spanish Inquisition start?

96 Here's a "Name Him" question. In the thirteenth century, this philosopher/scientist predicted the use of flying machines and power boats and foresaw the potency of gunpowder. Name him.

97 Name the famous book that was the first (c. 1454) to be printed using movable type.

98 What is the name of the Roman Catholic privy council charged with electing a new pope?

Answers

1 *The fall of the Western Roman Empire in 476 when Emperor Romulus Augustus died is most often cited as the beginning of the Middle Ages.*

2 *Richard I (1189–1199) was known as the Lion-Heart.*

③ *The Doomsday Book contained the results of a survey listing all landowners with the value and extent of their holdings. It was in part compiled to ensure tax collections.*

④ *It's the Cathedral of Notre Dame in Paris.*

⑤ *The magic implement was a cleft stick, a hayfork, or a shovel.*

⑥ *Breakspear was Pope Adrian IV. He made history, in fact, by being the only Englishman in history to attain that post.*

⑦ *All have the same middle name: Singh, which means lion.*

⑧ *The creche was originated by Saint Francis of Assisi (c. 1181–1226).*

⑨ *The first three Plantagenet kings of England, Henry II, Richard I, and John, were counts of Anjou. Thus, they were called Angevins, as well as Plantagenets.*

⑩ *The* Summa Theologica *was the work of Thomas Aquinas (1225–74), who was, in addition to being a philosopher, a Dominican friar.*

⑪ *Ghana was located between rich salt mines to the north and gold mines to the south.*

⑫ *Because of his father's travels to France Giovanni di Bernardone was later called Francesco; you would know him more by the name Saint Francis of Assisi.*

⑬ *They were attempting to create a drug that would ensure immortality, a long-life pill. Actually, this isn't as farfetched as it might seem. The ingredients used to produce "fire medicine," as gunpowder was labeled, were sulphur, saltpeter, and charcoal, all of which were used separately as medicines.*

⑭ *Mecca is the birthplace of Mohammed (c. 570 A.D.), in which the sacred shrine, called the Kaaba (or Ka'bah), is located. In the Kaaba is the* Black Stone, *which traditon says was given to Abraham by the angel Gabriel.*

⑮ *You're not going to believe this, but each is matched by its counterpart. 1. Britain = (a) Anglo-Saxons, 2. Italy = (b) Ostrogoths, 3. North Africa = (c) Vandals, and 4. Spain = (d) Visigoths.*

⑯ *Alaric's warriors diverted the River Busento, buried their fallen leader in the riverbed, then returned the water to its original channel, thus burying their king beneath the currents.*

⑰ *Paper money was first used in China, printed with copper plates and engraved with intricate designs to thwart counterfeiters.*

⑱ Tenochtitlán, *the site of present-day Mexico City, means "Place of the Prickly-pear Cactus," thus fulfilling a prophecy that they would settle in a swampy land where there would be an eagle on a prickly-pear cactus clutching a serpent in its beak.*

⑲ *The seven deadly sins are anger, covetousness (or greed), envy, gluttony, lust, pride, and sloth (or laziness).*

⑳ *The word evolved from the Arabic word "hashshashin," which means "eaters of hashish." The drug-crazed Assassin Sect was used against early Christians in the Crusades.*

㉑ *Mohammed (571–632 A.D.) founded the Muslim faith.*

㉒ *The hegira was the name for the 622 A.D. flight of Mohammed and his 200 followers from Mecca to Medina to escape persecution.*

㉓ *Four wives.*

㉔ *Purdah is the seclusion of women, which includes the wearing of veils.*

㉕ *They are the Sunnite Muslims and the Shiite Muslims. The division came about due to disputes over the succession to the caliphate, or rulership, of Islam.*

㉖ *Sentenced to die at dawn, Scheherazade tells one story per night, but leaves the ending for the following day, thus precluding the sentence being carried out. At the end of* One Thousand and One Nights *she is given a reprieve.*

㉗ *The Turkish forces were commanded by Saladin, or Salah-al-Din.*

㉘ *It was the marriage of Ferdinand of Aragon and Isabella of Castile. You would know them better as the financial backers of Christopher Columbus' expedition to what turned out to be the New World.*

㉙ *The Ottoman Turks had settled in Turkey centuries before they began their territorial expansion, but they were originally from Mongolia.*

㉚ *They were Germanic tribes from northeastern Germany.*

㉛ *William the Conqueror's assault took place in 1066.*

㉜ *No. The word Valhalla (or Walhalla) means hall of the slain. It is only for slain heroes.*

㉝ *No. The serfs were not slaves, but the nobles owned a portion of the fruits of the serfs' land, could claim a portion of their time, and could forbid them from leaving the estate.*

③④ *Starting in 1095, there were nine Crusades, the last being in 1271–72.*

③⑤ *Geoffrey of Monmouth.*

③⑥ *Excalibur.*

③⑦ *The true knights, as we have come to know these warriors, originated in France. They weren't introduced into England until the Norman Conquest.*

③⑧ *A bicameral parliament is a two-house legislature.*

③⑨ *They were Norsemen, or Northmen, from Denmark, Norway, and Sweden, who launched invasions by sea into other European lands.*

④⓪ *We call them troubadours. They were the knightly poets of their day.*

④① *The sons of knights were interned to another knight as pages or varlets. At about the age of fourteen they became esquires, or squires, the final step on their way to donning the armor of knighthood.*

④② *It was a flammable mixture, probably of naphtha, quicklime, and sulphur, that could be hurled in earthen pots at the enemy's structure, then ignited by a flaming arrow.*

(43) *Saint Thomas à Becket (1118–70) was archbishop of Canterbury.*

(44) *It marked the first time gunpowder was used in a battle in Europe.*

(45) *The Strait of Gibraltar, separating Europe and Africa at the mouth of the Mediterranean, is eight miles wide at its narrowest point, which separates Point Marroqui (Spain) and Point Cires (Morocco).*

(46) *The Ostrogoths were the East Goths, and the Visigoths were the West Goths.*

(47) *It was the Justinian Code, named for Justinian I, during whose reign the codification was completed.*

(48) *It was a form of bubonic plague. It was often termed the Black Plague, or Black Death, because in one form of the disease the hemorrhages turn black.*

(49) *The epidemic was transmitted to humans from rats by way of fleas.*

(50) *It was Saint Gregory VII, who was pope from 1073 to 1085.*

(51) *It was (c) Constantine (c. 288–337 A.D.). The phrase, often seen in its Latin form,* In hoc signo vinces, *is quoted in Eusebius'* Life of Constantine.

(52) *Khan's forces used the first true rockets, arrows launched by gunpowder.*

(53) *The crime of which Joan of Arc was convicted was heresy. She was placed on trial and declared to be guilty by French clerics who supported the British. The English carried out the execution.*

(54) *She led a small French force to victory over the British troops at the Battle of Orleans, thus earning her that nickname.*

(55) *The monks did a lot of copying of early books, thereby preserving these works for future generations.*

(56) *The world's first newspaper was published in Peking, China, during the T'ang Dynasty.*

(57) *Until around 600* A.D. *women had a great deal of influence in Japanese society. The Confucian philosophy ended that and women became subservient.*

(58) *He went to Ireland as a captive of Gaels at the age of sixteen (c. 405) and was sold into slavery.*

(59) *King John formalized the Magna Carta on June 19, 1215.*

(60) *The 719-year-old Leaning Tower (begun in 1173; completed in 1271) is 180 feet tall.*

(61) *The British used foot soldiers wielding longbows against the less mobile, heavily armored French knights on horseback.*

(62) Islam *means surrender, or submit, to Allah's will.*

(63) *Pictures, statues, and the like depicting human beings are forbidden in mosques.*

(64) *He has been romanticized over the centuries as Charlemagne (c. 742–814).*

(65) *The accolade was a touch or a blow on the shoulder or the neck either with a fist or a sword that dubbed the recipient a knight.*

(66) *Knights were awarded points for striking a blow with their lances. A hit in the helmet earned the highest points, but hitting "below the belt," as in today's prize fights, was a foul.*

(67) *From the white cliffs of its coast, Britain was originally named Albion.*

(68) *They were on their way to pay homage to Thomas à Becket, the famed archbishop of Canterbury.*

69 *Lady Godiva (c. 1040–80) made her famed ride (a) to protest oppressive taxation in (b) the town of Coventry.*

70 *The members of guilds were self-employed artisans, whereas today's union members are employees.*

71 *King John was blind. He was found with his horse's reins attached to the knights who had led him into battle.*

72 *At the behest of Emperor Alexius Comnenus of the Byzantine Empire, the pope proclaimed a Holy War to try to stem the advance of the Muslims. The proclamation resulted in the First Crusade (1096–99).*

73 *The male knight is* sir. *The woman is* dame.

74 *The "Children's Crusade" was actually a two-part tragedy. In the first a French shepherd, Stephen of Cloyes, led some 30,000 children, twelve years old and younger, ending in thousands of deaths along the trail and enslavement for countless others. This was repeated in an effort by some 20,000 more children led by a German boy named Nicholas. Most perished by hunger and disease.*

75 *Richard was captured by Leopold II of Austria in 1192, then turned over to*

Emperor Henry VI of Germany. He was released in 1194.

⑯ Pope *means father.*

⑰ *It is the Japanese code called* bushido, *or the* way of the warrior.

⑱ *It* was not *called the slave dynasty because it established slavery, it was thus labeled because Aybeh and some of his successors were former military slaves.*

⑲ *It was Greek fire, a substance that ignited upon contact with water. The flammable chemical was quite effective. As noted in an earlier question, Greek fire was also used quite effectively against castle fortresses.*

⑳ *The Knights of Saint John were to provide for the sick and wounded, while the Knights Templar protected the pilgrims.*

㉑ *Quite understandably, only three sets of the 11,100-volume* Great Encyclopedia *were produced. You see, the monumental work was handwritten.*

㉒ *The first Crusader ruler of Jerusalem was Godfrey of Bouillon, who became somewhat legendary by being included in the* Chansons De Geste, *a series of medieval French epic poems.*

(83) *The yeoman warders carry halberts or halberds, which have a long spike with an axe blade and sharp hook on a long shaft.*

(84) *The posted newspapers were called gazettas, because the public had to pay a gazetta if they wanted to read them.*

(85) *The Chinese ruler was Kublai Khan (c. 1216–94).*

(86) *Those ancient Chinese noodles were the forerunners to spaghetti, which so many of us think of as an Italian original.*

(87) *The shogun was a general appointed by the emperor to control the military. The shoguns eventually became more powerful than the emperors and actually ruled Japan for several centuries.*

(88) *They were Caucasian.*

(89) *(a) The Hanseatic League was a powerful federation of the towns in northern Germany, which was formed in 1358 as a commercial alliance. In fact, that's what the name means. (b) It's derived from the word* hansa, *meaning a defensive alliance.*

(90) *Having survived the onslaughts of the Persians, the Seljuk Turks, and the Crusaders over the centuries, the Byzantine empire fell to the Ottoman Turks in 1453.*

⑨⑴ *If the ruler was either too young or too incapacitated to manage the affairs of the kingdom, the power was instilled in either an administrator (regent) or a council.*

⑨⑵ *The Tartars were led by Genghis Khan (1162–1227).*

⑨⑶ *The Inquisition was, for the most part, aimed at forcing religious conformity, initially against Moors and Jews, but later encompassing Protestants.*

⑨⑷ *As inquisitor general under Ferdinand and Isabella in 1478, Tomas de Torquemada claimed that the presence of Jews in Spain was the main cause of Christians' backsliding.*

⑨⑸ *Although we often term it the Spanish Inquisition, it originated in Rome in 1233 under Pope Gregory IX. It was revived in Spain in 1479. Inquisitions were prevalent throughout Catholic Europe over a wide period of time.*

⑨⑹ *The man who was so ahead of his time was Roger Bacon (c. 1214–94).*

⑨⑺ *It was the* Gutenberg Bible, *which took its name from the inventor of movable (reusable) printing type, Johannes Gutenberg.*

⑨⑻ *The College of Cardinals is responsible for selecting the pope.*

Wanderlust Sets In

Following the Middle Ages, the European nations caught a severe case of wanderlust. Much of the urge for far horizons was motivated by the desire to open more areas to trade, especially the vast and lucrative areas of the Far East. The side effect of this was that it led to the discovery of the fertile lands of the Western Hemisphere, the South Pacific, and Africa.

Let's set sail on this journey into the new worlds.

① Prince Henry of Portugal (1394–1460) is known to history as Henry the Navigator. How did he earn that distinction?

② Early Spanish explorers of the New World referred to the country in question as the "rich coast." In fact, when Christopher Columbus landed off its shores in 1502, he was offered gifts of gold by the native Americans. Can you name the country?

3 Early explorers named this body of water the Great South Sea. By what name do we know the Great South Sea?

4 In the 1480s a Portuguese ship paved the way for a sea course to the Far East by rounding the Cape of Good Hope—the southern tip of Africa. Who was the navigator who commanded that excursion?

5 Following in the wake of the navigator in the preceding question was another Portuguese seaman, who rounded the Cape of Good Hope about a dozen years later and continued on to Calicut in Hindustan. Name this mariner.

6 To the early European traders the promised land for lucrative goods was Cathay. By what name do we know Cathay?

7 The book *Utopia* (1516) described communal land ownership, equal education for both sexes (a concept shocking in that time in history), and religious toleration. Who authored *Utopia*?

8 Here's a "Name Him" question. After having resettled in New York in

1696, this British subject was hired by the governor of the colony to engage in piracy against French ships. In later years he turned his piratic skills against British ships in the Indian Ocean. He climaxed his plundering by being tried and hung in his homeland. Name him.

9 Early explorers of the New World found three very advanced civilizations (compared to most of the native Americans). They were the Aztecs, the Incas, and the Mayans. In what modern-day country were each of these nations located?

10 If either Roger Bacon (1214–1292) or Leonardo da Vinci (1452–1519) had succeeded in perfecting an ornithopter, it would have been a boon to the early explorers. What is an *ornithopter*?

11 In 1790 Pitcairn Island in the South Pacific was settled by a group of British mariners. These sailors are well-known to modern movie-goers. Why?

12 Here's a "Name Him" question. One of the early would-be settlers of the New World, who has come down through history as a model of chivalry, was beheaded by order of King James I. He's entombed in Saint Margaret's Church near London's famed Westminster Abbey. Name him.

13 In 1519 Ferdinand Magellan set sail with a fleet of five ships to circumnavigate the globe. When did he complete the mission, and how many ships were left at the end of the journey?

14 Magellan discovered and laid claim to the Philippines during his globe-rounding trip. What nation's flag was planted on the Philippines?

15 Many of the early explorers met their Maker under cruel conditions. Which of the early explorers of North America was the victim of a mutiny, and set adrift in 1611 in an open boat, along with his son, to die?

16 Australia's early settlement was quite heavily spiced with shipments of convicts from England. Where were these prisoners sent before Australia became a "penal colony"?

17 An error by Martin Waldseemuller in 1507 has had a permanent effect on history and geography. What was Waldseemuller's goof?

18 When we think of tulips, we almost automatically think of Holland. But the tulip didn't "arrive" in Holland until the mid-sixteenth century. In what country did the flower originate?

19 Montezuma was one of the most important native American leaders encountered by the early Spanish explorers of the New World. Here's a two-part question for you: (a) Of what Indian nation was Montezuma the ruler, and (b) who was the Spanish explorer who captured Montezuma?

20 To what was Francisco de Coronado referring in 1541 when he reported to the king of Spain: "It is impossible to number them, for while I was journeying through these [Texas] plains . . . there was not a day that I lost sight of them"?

21 We often hear about Manhattan being purchased from its Indian inhabitants for twenty-four dollars worth of trinkets. (Some say the tribe that sold it to the representatives of the Dutch West India Company didn't really own it.) Who was the leader of the European delegation that made the purchase?

22 The Dutch who settled in South Africa in the mid-1600s were dubbed *Boers*. What was the origin of this label?

23 Who first brought tobacco and the potato to England from the New World?

24 How many days did it take Christopher Columbus to cross the Atlantic and anchor at the land he believed to be India?

25 What was the *caravel*, which was of such importance to early explorations?

26 What nation pioneered the trade by which so many Africans were sold and pressed into centuries of slavery in the New World?

27 The vice admiral of the British naval forces in the battle against the Spanish Armada made a name for himself by his earlier attacks against Spanish colonies in the New World. He also was the first Englishman to circumnavigate the globe. Who was this noted mariner?

28 During the Ming Dynasty (1368–1643) the Chinese were bothered by what they termed the *ocean devils*. What were the ocean devils?

29 Hawaii was first opened to the West by a British explorer in 1778. Name that famed sea captain.

30 It's time for a "Match 'em" question. In the left-hand column, "The Answer Man" will give you the name of a sailing vessel. Your chore is to match it with the expedition in the right-hand column in which that craft played a role.

Ship	Expedition
1. *Half Moon*	(a) Discovery of the New World
2. *Mayflower*	(b) Exploration of Hudson Bay
3. *Santa Maria*	(c) First circumnavigation of the globe
4. *Susan Constant*	(d) Settlement of Jamestown Colony
5. *Vittoria*	(e) Settlement of Plymouth Colony

31 John Cabot was commissioned by Henry VII to sail to the New World in 1497 and on his voyage he discovered Newfoundland. What nationality was Cabot?

32 Who discovered the Saint Lawrence River in 1534?

33 John Cabot's expedition to Newfoundland resulted in a discovery that led to the first major item of export for the New England area. What was that important commercial commodity?

34 Quebec, Canada, has long been a city strongly influenced by descendants of its early French settlers. Here's a two-part question for you: (a) Who led the French expedition that first settled Quebec, and (b) in what year was that settlement established?

35 When Sir Francis Drake circumnavigated the globe (1577–80) he began his journey on the *Pelican*, but returned to port on the *Golden Hind*. What happened to the *Pelican*?

36 Did Columbus ever become aware that he had discovered a New World?

37 We read much about pirates and their adventures on the Spanish Main. Where is the Spanish Main?

38 Greenland is not exactly a tropical paradise. Where did it get its unusual (considering its climate) name?

39 It wasn't until 1542, fully a half-century after Columbus' expedition to the New World, that the first European traders found their way to Japan. What was the nationality of these merchant seamen who landed on this island-nation?

40 Many of the early explorers of the New World suffered sad fates for their efforts. The conquistador who discovered and laid claim to the Pacific Ocean in the name of Spain in 1513 was later accused of treason and beheaded. Who was this ill-fated explorer?

41 Related to the preceding query, among the Spanish conquistadors who discovered the Pacific was a man who in 1532 conquered Peru. His fate was assassination by one of his fellow explorers. His bones are kept in a glass case in a cathedral in Lima, which he founded as Peru's capital. Can you name this early visitor to South America?

42 Much of the opening of new territories by way of exploration came about due to the search for the Northeast and Northwest passages. These search missions increased greatly after 1453. What caused these stepped-up efforts to open new waterways?

43 Dutch, Portuguese, and Spanish ships sighted Australia in the 1600s, but the territory was finally claimed as a British possession in 1770. Who was the famed sea captain who staked that claim?

44 The first European explorer to open the Southwestern area of what was to one day become the United States did so while searching for the fabled Seven Cities of Cibola. Who was this frustrated founder?

45 A major find in 1911 was a 400-year-old fortress-city, believed to have been used by the Incas as a defense against enemy intruders. What is the name of this mountain fortress?

46 In c. 1483, Diogo Cao, a Portugese navigator, made an important discovery in Africa. What did Cao discover?

47 One of the changes wrought on the European countries by the expanded explorations and the discoveries of new trade items was the birth of widespread mercantilism. What is mercantilism?

48 The funding of early exploration, such as that provided by the Dutch East India and West India companies, led to the spreading of financial risk among many backers. What form of company was created to provide this capital?

49 The Ashanti Empire played a key role in international trade in the 1700s. What commodity did the empire supply to British and Dutch merchants?

50 It was no ill-wind that blew Pedro Cabral's vessel off course in 1500. Cabral, a Portugese navigator, headed for India, but was blown westward where he laid claim to a New World possession. Over what future country did Portugal gain dominion as a result of Cabral's misdirection?

51 In 1517 a trade agreement, called the *Asiento*, was signed between a Genoese company and the Spanish crown. What was the object to be supplied by the Genoese company?

52 What was the major importance of spices from the Far East to the early Europeans?

Answers

① *Prince Henry established a school and observatory to train seamen, which did much for the opening of navigational routes to the Far East.*

② *The hint was in the question if you read it carefully: The explorers called it "rich coast," or* Costa Rica. *Columbus thought he had landed in Asia near Siam.*

③ *The Great South Sea is now known as the Pacific Ocean.*

④ *The journey was navigated by Bartolomeo Diaz (sometimes spelled Bartholomeu Dias).*

⑤ *Vasco da Gama was the first to sail to India around the Cape.*

⑥ *Cathay is the land we know as China.*

⑦ Utopia *was written by Sir Thomas More (1478–1535).*

⑧ *His name was William Kidd (c. 1645–1701). You'd know him better as Captain Kidd.*

⑨ *Both the Aztec and Mayan civilizations were in what is now Mexico. The Inca nation was in present-day Peru.*

⑩ *It's a manned aircraft operated by the flapping of its wings.*

⑪ *The settlers were the men whose exploits were immortalized in* Mutiny on the Bounty. *They were the mutineers of H.M.S.* Bounty *fame.*

⑫ *He's Sir Walter Raleigh, whose attempt at settling the New World resulted in the Lost Colony in what is now North Carolina. You may recall the story of Raleigh placing his cape in a puddle so Queen Elizabeth I would not get her slippers wet.*

⑬ *Magellan never completed the trip. He was killed by natives in the Philippines. The surviving crew of eighteen, under the command of Sebastian del Cano, arrived home in the lone remaining ship in September 1522.*

⑭ *Although Magellan was a Portuguese nobleman, he was sailing under the flag of Spain, in whose name he claimed the Philippines.*

⑮ *The ill-fated explorer was Henry Hudson, who was set adrift in 1611.*

⑯ *Some forty-thousand English and Irish prisoners were sold into slavery on America's plantations.*

⑰ *Martin Waldseemuller recorded the New World as "America," saying Amerigo (or Americus) Vespucci (1454–1512) had discovered it.*

⑱ *The tulip was brought to Holland from Turkey.*

⑲ *(a) Montezuma (1466–1520) was the ruler of the Aztecs of central Mexico. (b) He was captured by Hernan Cortes (sometimes spelled Hernando Cortez). He was killed either by the Spanish or his own rebellious people. No one knows for sure which.*

⑳ *Coronado was reporting on the herds of American bison, or, as we often call them, buffalo.*

㉑ *Peter Minuit led the expedition that resulted in the purchase of Manhattan in 1626.*

㉒ Boer *is the Dutch word for farmer or husbandman.*

㉓ *They were introduced by Sir Walter Raleigh (1552–1618).*

(24) *The crossing took thirty-six days from the Canary Islands; seventy from Spain.*

(25) *The caravel was a ship designed by the Portuguese in the fifteenth century. It was compact and seaworthy for long voyages.*

(26) *By the mid-1600s, the Dutch, who had taken over the control of the African Gold Coast from the Portuguese, instituted the purchase of African natives from African tribal leaders.*

(27) *The British navigator was Sir Francis Drake (1540?–96).*

㉘ *The ocean devils were the Europeans. It seems some European traders, especially the Portugese, had presented a poor image in the minds of the Chinese.*

㉙ *Captain James Cook discovered the Sandwich Islands, which we know as Hawaii.*

㉚ *1(b) The* Half Moon *was Henry Hudson's ship in his exploration of the Hudson River and Bay; 2(e) the* Mayflower *was the Pilgrims' ship in their journey to Plymouth; 3(a) the* Santa Maria *was Columbus' main ship in his discovery of the New World; 4(d) the* Susan Constant *was one of three ships used to bring settlers to Jamestown; and 5(c) the* Vittoria *was the only one of Magellan's ships to complete the trip around the world.*

㉛ *Giovanni Caboto (Cabot's real name) was a Venetian.*

㉜ *Jacques Cartier, by commission of King Francis I of France, explored the Saint Lawrence River and its estuaries.*

㉝ *Cabot discovered codfish, which became a major supply source for the British Navy.*

㉞ *(a) The expedition, under Samuel de Champlain, (b) established Quebec in 1608.*

③⑤ *The only thing that happened to the* Pelican *is that it underwent a name change during the voyage. The* Pelican *and the* Golden Hind *were the same ship.*

③⑥ *No. Columbus died thinking he had found a new route to Asia.*

③⑦ *It's the northern coast of South America.*

③⑧ *Eric the Red gave Greenland its name (c. 982) when he founded it as a self-governing colony. He named it for its green coastlines rather than its icy interior in an effort to lure settlers.*

③⑨ *The Portuguese opened trade with Japan and had a virtual monopoly on it for another half-century, before Spanish, then Dutch and English traders followed.*

④⓪ *Vasco Nunez de Balboa (c. 1475–1519)*

④① *The ill-fated Spanish conquistador was Francisco Pizarro (c. 1476–1541).*

④② *It was during this period when the Turks took control over the well-known land routes to the Far East.*

④③ *Captain James Cook.*

㊹ *The Spanish explorer Francisco Vasquez de Coronado (c. 1510–54).*

㊺ *You may visit Machu Picchu if you travel to Peru. The name, Machu Picchu, means "place to which the sun was tied."*

㊻ *The Congo River, which wasn't traced to its source until Sir Henry Stanley of Great Britain explored it in 1877.*

㊼ *Mercantilism is a form of protectionist trade system, adopted by most of the European countries.*

㊽ *These were joint-stock companies in which shareholders split the profits and the risks.*

㊾ *The Ashanti, which ruled the part of Africa that is now central Ghana, supplied slaves seized from those people they had conquered.*

㊿ *Cabral's trip ended up in Brazil. Brazil is the only South American country that derives its culture and language from Portugal.*

㉛ *Under the* Asiento de negroes *(the full name of the contract), the Genoese company was to supply 1,000 slaves over an eight-year period to the Spanish colonies.*

㉜ *Spices were used not just to flavor food, but also to help preserve it.*

The Rise of the Modern World

Once most of the world was opened—insofar as access via navigation was concerned—the more-advanced nations began to consolidate the various territories. This led to the establishment of those nations that would develop the world. It also brought conflict between the nations vying for control over some of the newly accessible territories. Naturally, there would be changes in the ensuing years in the forms of government under which the diverse nations would operate, and there would be additional border changes, but these, for the most part, would be less dramatic than those that occurred during this era.

❶ One of history's most fascinating periods was the Renaissance, which extended over a three-century period (1400–1700). What does the word *Renaissance* mean?

❷ Here's a "Name Her" question. This German princess married the heir to the throne of a European country. When her husband took the throne and mistreated her, she won over the imperial guard, had herself named empress, and forced her husband to abdicate. He was later executed. Name her.

❸ This one will really tax your knowledge of history: What is unique about the period between October 4, 1582, and October 15, 1582?

❹ The two nations located on the Iberian Peninsula figured prominently in the rise of the modern nations. Can you name these two countries?

❺ The red and white striped barber's pole symbolized the early services in addition to haircutting performed in these shops. What were those services?

❻ One of the Christian sects in the Protestant Reformation was known as the Anabaptists. Where did they get their name?

7 Dr. Edward Jenner (1749–1823) discovered that people working with cows caught a mild disease called cowpox, but never caught smallpox. So he injected patients with cowpox, then exposed them to smallpox and found they were immune. Why did this process come to be called "vaccination?"

8 We often hear reference to the Black Hole of Calcutta. What was the Black Hole?

9 In 1588 a famous naval confrontation occurred wherein a 197-ship force defeated a 130-ship opponent. Can you name the two forces?

10 In 1543 Nicholas Copernicus (1473–1543) upset the Ptolemaic theory regarding the sun and the earth. What was that original theory?

11 The doctrine of *Divine Right* reached its high-water mark in seventeenth-century Europe. What was *Divine Right*?

12 One of history's most extensive empires was that ruled by Akbar (1556–1605). Of what kingdom was Akbar the ruler?

13 King Henry VIII of England (1491–1547) would have fit in well with some of our multimarried present-day celebrities, but for the method the monarch used to shed his wives. Here's a two-part question for you. (a) How many times was Henry married, and (b) how many of his wives were beheaded?

14 Probably the most famous opera composed by Modest Mussorgsky (or Moussorsky), the famed Russian composer, was *Boris Godunov*. Who was Boris Godunov?

15 One of the most popular U.S. backyard games was born in France in the seventeenth century. Can you name it?

16 The city of Helsinki was founded in 1550 by King Gustavus I of Sweden, but it's not Sweden's capital. Name the country whose capital is Helsinki.

17 In 1712 John Arbuthnot, a Scottish author-physician, created a character in a series of pamphlets that has become a symbol of the British citizenry similar to our Uncle Sam. Who is that character?

18 Many of the world's societies over the centuries have been governed by systems of gerontocracy. What is gerontocracy?

19 While Americans have more or less officially been observing Mother's Day for over a half-century, it is not unique to dedicate a special day to mothers. The British had what was called Mothering Sunday. Do you know what this was?

20 England's famed Virgin Queen, Queen Elizabeth I (1533–1603), was declared to be an illegitimate child. Why?

21 This famed architect was responsible for many of England's most cherished structures, especially houses of worship. The inscription on his tomb in Saint Paul's Cathedral in London reads: "Si monumentum requiris, circumspice," which translates as "If you seek [my] monument, look around you." Who is this astronomer-turned-architect? (Hint: There's a touch of him in Williamsburg, Virginia.)

22 In the middle of the seventeenth century one of the signs of change in Europe was the dissolution of the Holy Roman Empire, which had dominated much of Europe since the early Middle Ages. In what country was the Holy Roman Empire centered?

23 Name the ruling family of France from the late sixteenth century until the French Revolution.

24 A Jesuit visiting Japan in the mid-1500s made note of the difference between Japanese castles and those in the Western countries. A major difference was the use of curves and the lack of mortar to bind the stones. Japanese castles used small stones to bind the large stones together. Why was this unique construction necessary?

25 A goodly number of plays were produced in Great Britain during the period known as the Restoration (1660–88). Why were so many stage productions created in that particular period of history?

26 Many of Shakespeare's plays were based on real people and events, such as *Julius Caesar*. Were (a) *Macbeth* and (b) *Romeo and Juliet* based on fact or fiction?

27 Niccolo Machiavelli, who gave us the word *Machiavellian* to denote unscrupulous behavior, is best known for *The Prince*. What famed person is believed to have inspired the work?

28 The famed catacombs, threading beneath the streets of Rome, were discovered in 1598. What was the main purpose for which these underground passages were constructed?

29 In 1598 French Protestants were granted religious freedom and full civil rights. What was the name of the declaration granting these rights?

30 Who is considered the founder of modern philosophy? His basic tenet is that truth in secular matters can only be found by the use of reason.

31 In the Battle of Mons, William III, prince of Orange (1650–1702), was saved from being victimized by Spanish raiders by Kuntze. Who was Kuntze?

32 How did the House of Hanover take over the British throne from the Stuarts in 1714?

33 Name the ruler of the Ottoman Empire who was called "the Magnificent" and "the Lawmaker." During his reign as sultan (1520–66), his naval forces conquered Belgrade, Rhodes, southern Hungary, and parts of Persia, Iraq, and Tripoli.

34 Henry VI's reign in England was marked by turmoil, including the Wars of the Roses. How old was Henry VI when he ascended to the throne of England in 1422?

35 The *Encyclopaedia Britannica* is probably the most famous research book in the world. When was the first *Britannica* published? And, for extra credit, how many volumes did it include?

36 Agra is the site of the tomb Shah Jahan erected for his wife. By what name do we know this tomb to Jahan's loved one?

37 The Russian Empire waived taxes for a band of warriors from its southern regions in exchange for service as scouts and cavalry. Who were these tribesmen who sprang up in the sixteenth century?

38 The first king of England of the House of Hanover was a German who rarely visited Great Britain and never even learned the language. Name this absentee monarch.

39 What French king was called the *Sun King*?

40 Under Peter the Great (1685–1725), the capital of Russia was switched from Moscow (its present capital) to a new location. What city was Russia's capital during Peter the Great's reign?

41 Where did the Puritans get their name?

42 In 1774 Joseph Priestly, an English clergyman, discovered the element in the atmosphere that is necessary for sustaining combustion. What element did Priestly discover?

43 Where did we get the modern term *Star Chamber* proceedings, describing unfair or arbitrary courtroom procedures?

44 Galileo is renowned for constructing the telescope and opening new worlds in the heavens. What was Galileo's full name?

45 Who was the first queen of England?

46 Speaking of women heads of state, has China ever had a woman ruler?

47 British Prime Minister Robert Walpole (1676–1745) was known for his efforts to establish Great Britain's foreign trade and keep the nation out of war. But he was also known for setting a precedent. What was that *first* established by Robert Walpole, earl of Orford?

48 What modern card game derived from the seventeenth-century game of Whist?

49 Led by Saint Ignatius of Loyola (1491–1556) the Jesuits became a powerful force in the Catholic battle against the Reformation forces and grew to be the largest religious order in modern times. What was Ignatius' original occupation prior to his becoming a religious leader?

50 "Though God hath raised me high, yet this I count the glory of my crown: that I have reigned with your loves." Who Said It: (a) Catherine II of Russia, (b) Elizabeth I of England, (c) Mary I of England, or (d) Isabella I of Spain?

51 In 1704 Alexander Selkirk was set ashore on the Juan Fernandez Islands in the South Pacific by his ship's captain. This is believed to have inspired the famed book *Robinson Crusoe*. Here's your question. Who wrote *Robinson Crusoe*? And, what was the novel's full title?

52 In early England, the yeomen of the guard were the sovereigns' bodyguards. What was another name by which these yeomen were known? (Hint: The name is borne by an alcoholic beverage on the market today.)

53 While many planets could be observed with the naked eye, in 1781 William Herschel, using a telescope, made the first discovery of a planet in recorded history. What planet did Herschel sight?

54 The Central Criminal Court in London is called Old Bailey. Where did that name originate?

55 Starting from the late 1600s there were two political parties in Britain. Can you name them?

56 What two kingdoms comprised the Kingdom of the Two Sicilies?

57 Who was the first ruler of Russia to adopt the title of czar in 1547?

58 Catherine of Aragon, Henry VIII's first wife, was divorced by the king because she failed to produce a male heir. Who were Catherine's parents?

59 The Royal Highlanders, a Scottish infantry regiment formed in 1739, is better-known by what name?

60 When was the first recorded mention of the concept of using contact lenses?

61 The word stationary comes to us from the *stationarii*, or booksellers, of old. Why were they referred to as stationary?

62 The ongoing battle between the Puritans and the Roman Catholic Church resulted in Queen Elizabeth I's *via media* (middle way) solution. What resulted from the *via media*?

63 Talk about advancing science, this English mathematician and natural philosopher discovered the law of gravity and the fact that white light contains all the colors of the spectrum. Name him.

64 Pope Leo X (1475–1521) raised a controversy by selling *indulgences* to help fund the rebuilding of Saint Peter's Basilica in Rome. What is an indulgence?

65 The first book on farming to be published in England in 1523 recommended *mixed farming*. What is mixed farming?

66 Here's a "Name Him" question. He was a professor of theology at the University of Wittenberg, who was accused of writing heretical books and undermining the authority of the Church. When he refused to recant, following the Diet of Worms, he was excommunicated. Name him.

67 The Louvre in Paris is one of the world's most famous art museums, housing such works as the *Mona Lisa* and the *Venus de Milo*. What was the original purpose of the building?

68 One of the innovations in seventeenth-century warfare was chain shot. What made chain shot different from the normal cannonball?

69 Upon hearing the word telephone we immediately envision the instrument that either bugs us by ringing when we're busy, or is tied up by a teenager when we want to use it. But Alexander Graham Bell's electronic marvel was not the first implement to be called a telephone. Can you guess what device was?

70 When we think of the Renaissance, the artistic achievements of the period immediately come to mind. There was, however, an accounting innovation that has greatly affected the generations to this very day. What was this bookkeeping invention?

71 Martin Luther is the founder of the Lutheran Church, but can you name the man who founded the Presbyterian Church?

72 In 1534 the king of England broke with the Roman Catholic Church because the pope refused to allow him to divorce his wife. Who was this monarch?

73 How did England come to be known as Great Britain?

74 Many U.S. cities with high concentrations of Scottish descendants hold annual Scottish games ceremonies. Can you name the game, believed to be of Scottish origin, that was introduced into London by King James I in the early 1600s?

75 Ivan IV of Russia, known to history as Ivan the Terrible, earned that nickname by a lifetime of cruel acts, including the murder of his own son, also named Ivan. Ivan started early by ordering the murder of one of his own *boyars* (nobles). How old was Ivan when he arranged this murder?

76 Armand Jean du Plessis virtually ruled France during the reign of Louis XIII. It was under his administration that the Huguenots, Protestant followers of Calvin, were stripped of their political power. By what name do we know du Plessis?

77 Daniel Gabriel Fahrenheit (1686–1736), a German physicist, was the first to use mercury in a thermometer (1714). What was used in thermometers prior to Fahrenheit's discovery?

78 In 1749 a government unit was created in England that came to be known by two names, the Bow Street Runners and the Robin Redbreasts. For what purpose were the Runners/Redbreasts created?

Answers

① Renaissance *is French for rebirth.*

② *It was Catherine II of Russia, known as Catherine the Great (1729–96).*

③ *What is unique is that it never occurred! There was no October 5 through 14, 1582. Pope Gregory XIII, for whom the Gregorian Calendar is named, ordered that Thursday, October 5 would be followed by Friday, October 14 in order to correct the errors in the previous calendars. Just think how many disappointed kids missed birthdays, and how many folks loved it—they missed a year's age.*

④ *Portugal and Spain comprise the Iberian Peninsula.*

⑤ *The early barbers were also surgeons.*

⑥ *The Anabaptists denied the validity of the baptism of infants. They advocated adult baptism.*

⑦ *The Latin word for cow is* vacca, *thus vaccination.*

⑧ *In 1756, during the Anglo-French fight for control of India, 146 British, including one woman, were captured by an Indian leader and placed overnight in an eighteen-foot-square cell. During the night 123 died. That cell became known as the Black Hole.*

⑨ *It was the British victory over the "invincible" Spanish Armada. The smaller, faster British ships harried the larger Spanish vessels. It should be noted that many Spanish ships were destroyed in a storm.*

⑩ *The Ptolemaic theory was that the sun and planets revolved around the earth. Copernicus said the planets, including the earth, revolved around the sun.*

(11) *Divine Right was the belief that a king's power came from God, and the ruler was thus accountable only to God.*

(12) *Akbar ruled the Mogul Empire, which extended from central Asia to southern India, and from Persia to the Ganges. One of his innovations was to include both Hindus and Moslems in his administration.*

(13) *(a) Six: Catharine of Aragon (widow of Henry's brother, Arthur), Anne Boleyn, Jane Seymour, Anne of Cleves, Catherine Howard, and Catherine Parr. (b) Two: Boleyn and Howard, were beheaded. He divorced Anne of Cleves, had his marriage to Catharine of Aragon declared invalid, and Seymour died in childbirth. He was still wed to Catherine Parr when he died.*

(14) *Godunov (c. 1551–1605) was czar of Russia from 1598 to 1605.*

(15) *It's croquet.*

(16) *Helsinki is the capital of Finland, not Sweden.*

(17) *He's known as John Bull, considered to be representative of the average British gentleman.*

(18) *Gerontocracy is government by a council of elders, or a governing body comprised of old men.*

⑲ *On the Mid-Lent Sunday, it was a custom for children who were apprenticed out, or had jobs as servants, to carry a small gift, or a "mothering cake," home to their mothers.*

⑳ *Elizabeth was the daughter of Anne Boleyn and King Henry VIII. She was declared illegitimate because the Catholic Church claimed that Henry was still married to Catherine of Aragon, his first wife.*

㉑ *The English architect is Christopher Wren (1632–1723).*

㉒ *It was centered in Germany, not in Rome, as one might think. The kings of Austria were usually the emperors of the Holy Roman Empire.*

㉓ *It was the Bourbons, whose most-famed monarchs were Louis XIV and Louis XVI.*

㉔ *It was necessary because the frequent earthquakes in Japan precluded rigid construction methods. Some of these castles have withstood earth tremors for over 400 years.*

㉕ *Plays had been banned under Oliver Cromwell's puritanical rule (1649–60), so once the ban was off there was an influx of plays presented.*

㉖ *(a)* Macbeth *was based on the exploits of Macbeth, a king of Scotland (1040–1057). (b)* Romeo and Juliet *were fictional characters.*

㉗ *It is believed that Cesare Borgia (1476–1507), an Italian cardinal and military leader, was the personna on whom* The Prince *was based. Borgia's father was Pope Alexander VI.*

㉘ *Although they were often used to hide away from the authorities, their main purpose was for use as burial sites.*

㉙ *The Edict of Nantes.*

㉚ *It was the French philosopher, René Descartes (1596–1650).*

㉛ *Kuntze was a white pug. The dog's alarm saved William of Orange.*

㉜ *When Queen Anne died heirless, under the terms of the Act of Settlement of 1701, the crown passed to the House of Hanover.*

㉝ *The sultan who ruled during this era of conquest was Suleiman I.*

㉞ *Henry VI was nine months old when he became king.*

㉟ *The initial* Encyclopaedia Britannica *three-volume—Yes, three volumes!—reference work was published in 1771.*

㊱ *The tomb is the Taj Mahal in Agra, India. It was constructed by some 20,000 workers between 1632 and 1653.*

㊲ *The Cossacks.*

㊳ *The first Hanover king was George I (1714–27).*

㊴ *It was Louis XIV (1643–1715), who is noted for the saying, "L'etat, c'est moi," which translates as "I am the state."*

㊵ *The capital under Peter the Great was Saint Petersburg.*

㊶ *It came from their desire to* purify *the Church of England.*

㊷ *Priestly discovered the existence of oxygen. Don't leave home without it.*

㊸ *The name comes from the royal court in England, where cases were held sans juries, and the decisions were decidedly weighted against the accused. They were finally abolished in 1641.*

㊹ *His name was Galileo Galilei (1564–1642).*

㊺ *Mary (1553–58) of the Tudor line was England's first queen.*

㊻ *Yes. In 683–705 A.D., Empress Wu Chao' ruled China upon the death of her husband, Emperor Kao T'ang/Tsung. Tz'u Hsi (1861–1908), as dowager empress, was one of the last hereditary rulers of China.*

㊼ *Walpole is regarded as the* first *of Great Britain's prime ministers.*

㊽ *The game of bridge.*

㊾ *Ignatius of Loyola, born of a noble family, was a soldier. His military career was disrupted by a severe wound and, while recovering, he conceived of the idea of becoming a "soldier for Christ."*

㊿ *The answer is (b). Elizabeth I is thus quoted by Chamberlin in* Sayings of Queen Elizabeth.

(51) *The full title of Daniel Defoe's work was* The Life and Strange Surprizing Adventures of Robinson Crusoe of York, Mariner. *That title alone is a short story.*

(52) *The yeomen of the guard were sometimes called beefeaters.*

(53) *The planet Herschel discovered was Uranus, the seventh furthest from the sun.*

(54) *The courtyards of old castles were called baileys. Old Bailey is on what was once the city's outer boundary wall.*

(55) *They were the Tory and Whig parties. The Whigs supported Parliament over the crown, while the Tories were aristocratic.*

(56) *Naples and Sicily, including all of southern Italy below the so-called Papal States, comprised the Kingdom of the Two Sicilies.*

(57) *Ivan IV, or Ivan the Terrible (1530–84), was the first czar.*

(58) *Catherine of Aragon's parents were Ferdinand and Isabella of Spain, who had commissioned Columbus' expedition to the New World.*

(59) *The Royal Highlanders are known as the Black Watch, a name derived from their dark kilts.*

(60) *Amazingly, Leonardo da Vinci (1452–1519) was the first person to record the concept. Da Vinci's reference came at the beginning of the sixteenth century.*

(61) *Most tradesmen traveled to sell their wares, but the booksellers operated*

for the most part from stationary sites, such as stalls or shops.

(62) *The* via media *resulted in the creation of the Anglican Church.*

(63) *An easy question. It was, of course, Sir Isaac Newton (1642–1727).*

(64) *An indulgence was a pardon freeing the recipient from some or all of the suffering in purgatory, the place between heaven and earth where a sinner was purified via some form of punishment for his or her earthly transgressions.*

(65) *Mixed farming means raising crops and livestock, as opposed to crops alone. The authors, Sir Anthony Fitzherbert and his brother John, caused a stir with their concept of agriculture.*

(66) *He was Martin Luther (1483–1546), whose posting of his Ninety-five Theses touched off the Protestant Reformation.*

(67) *The Louvre was built to be a palace. Most of the construction was completed during the reign of Louis XIV (1643–1715).*

(68) *Chain shot consisted of cannonballs linked by a chain. It was especially effective when fired at the rigging of enemy ships.*

(69) *In the late seventeenth century, the word* telephone *was used to describe the string telephones used by kids.*

(70) *Early in the fourteenth century, the Italians developed double-entry bookkeeping. By the fifteenth century it was used throughout Europe, greatly facilitating international trade.*

(71) *John Calvin (1509–64) founded the Presbyterian Church.*

(72) *Henry VIII.*

(73) *Under the act of union (1707), the separate governments of England and Scotland were combined, thus giving birth to Great Britain.*

(74) *Many a "Sunday widow" would love to get her hands on King James I for introducing the game of golf to the rest of the Anglo-Saxon world, from which it eventually migrated across the Atlantic.*

(75) *Ivan the Terrible (1530–84) was thirteen years old when he had Andrei Shuisky murdered.*

(76) *History knows du Plessis by his title, Cardinal Richelieu, or more correct, cardinal and duc de Richelieu (1585–1642).*

(77) *Early thermometers were filled with alcohol.*

(78) *A forerunner to the modern-day Criminal Investigation Department, the Bow Street Runners were an early detective force. Their names came respectively from the Bow Street Police Office in London, from which they operated, and their red waistcoats.*

Revolutionary Fever Spreads

Once the modern nations were, for the most part, established as far as their territorial limits were concerned, internal changes were inevitable. You might call it growing pains. Revolutions broke out, both in the distant territories, such as the American colonies, and the homelands themselves, as in France. It was an Age of Revolution, or perhaps, more appropriately, Evolution.

In addition to the revolutions involving battlefields, another, more peaceful, revolution began in England around 1750. This revolution involved inventors rather than generals. The Industrial Revolution, as it has come to be called, *lasted about 100 years and has had a profound, worldwide effect.*

❶ With the help of native rebel forces, the French in 1794 succeeded in driving the British and Spanish out of Haiti. Can you name the Haitian who led the rebels?

❷ In what country was the *ancien régime*, which was based on the theory of the absolute monarchy and the divine right of kings, ensconced until 1789? What caused its fall?

❸ The American colonies' break with Great Britain, in addition to giving birth to the United States, resulted in the founding of a major new religious group. Can you name it?

❹ On January 1, 1729, the author of *Reflections on the French Revolution* was born in Dublin. Name him.

❺ Can you name the three nations that eventually emerged from the country once known as El Gran Colombia? And, for extra credit, name the man who founded El Gran Colombia.

❻ When was the first successful parachute descent from an appreciable height (3,000 feet) made?

7 Who was Atahualpa?

8 An icon of the French revolution is the key to the Bastille. Where is this key currently on display?

9 The Bastille has been described as "a symbol of the despotism of the Bourbons." What exactly was the Bastille?

10 The guillotine was named after Joseph Ignace Guillotin, the Frenchman who first proposed its use as a means of execution. Do you know what Guillotin's occupation was?

11 History's first black republic was established in 1804. Can you name this ground-breaking country?

12 What was the name of the radical party led by Robespierre in the French Revolution?

13 One of the first cases of U.S. military forces being dispatched to a foreign country was the Tripolitan, or Barbary, Wars (1800–15) when troops and ships were sent into North Africa. What was the cause of that military action?

14 It was during the reign of George III that the American colonists got fed up, revolted, and formed the United States. How did

King George III finally end up losing all of his power?

⑮ The Industrial Revolution (roughly 1750–1850) saw inventions that brought the demise of much of the home (cottage) industries in favor of factories. In the first column are the names of inventors who had an effect on this revolution. Your task is to link them to the invention in the second column by which they contributed to the Industrial Revolution.

Inventor	Invention
1. Richard Arkwright	**(a)** Flying shuttle
2. Edmund Cartwright	**(b)** Power loom
3. Samuel Crompton	**(c)** Roller Spinning Frame
4. James Hargreave	**(d)** Spinning Jenny
5. John Kay	**(e)** Spinning Mule (muslin-wheel)

⑯ Name the American who, though not allowed back into the United States, was buried in his American uniform in Great Britain.

⑰ "I love the Americans because they love liberty, and I love them for the noble efforts they made in the last war." Who Said It: (a) Edmund Burke, (b) Samuel Johnson, (c) the Marquis de Lafayette, or (d) William Pitt?

18 The phrase "capital punishment" originated during the French Revolution. But it did not mean capital in the terms of being the ultimate punishment. Where did the expression come from?

19 This revolutionary figure was influential in freeing at least five South American countries from foreign rule. His goal was a united South America, but his dictatorial manner resulted in separatist movements. Name him.

20 The guillotine gained infamy for its use in the French Revolution. How long following the Revolution did it remain in use?

21 In what revolution did the period known as the "Reign of Terror" take place?

22 We're all familiar with our system of turnpikes. But where did the *turnpike* get its name?

23 The French and Indian War (1689–1763) in the American colonies was actually part of another war in Europe. What was the European war called?

24 There's a rather small colony of Barbary apes on the Rock of Gibraltar, which is a British possession, although the United

Nations has requested that Britain end its sovereignty by 1996. Do you know the legend that is associated with these furry inhabitants of the Rock?

㉕ During the "age of revolution" a unique type of lawbreaker gained some prominence. The Australians called them *bushrangers*, but what is the more widely known name for these criminals?

㉖ Until the Revolution of 1789, this Protestant group, which originated in Switzerland following the teachings of John Calvin, was greatly persecuted in France. Many fled the country. Can you name them?

㉗ What two European imperialistic powers controlled most of Latin America when revolutionary fever broke out there between 1791 and 1824?

㉘ In 1825 Juan Lavalleja led a group known as the "Thirty-three Immortals" in a move to form an independent nation. What new country was created, and from what country did they secede?

㉙ Aurangzeb, the last Mogul emperor to control all of India (1658–1707), lost his kingdom because of his fanaticism. What particular policy caused the revolt against Aurangzeb?

30 In 1850 an uprising broke out in China, led by Hung Hsiu-ch'uan, who claimed to be the brother of Jesus. At one point the rebel army numbered one million. Although the rebellion was broken and Hung committed suicide, this outburst is seen as a precursor to the later breakup of China between the Nationalists and the Communists. By what name is this revolution known?

31 Here's a "Name Him" question. This Polish count, a key figure in the 1768 revolt against Russia, was sent into exile. He moved to America where he died leading his cavalry unit against the British forces in Savannah, Georgia, in the Revolutionary War. Name him.

32 In 1793 both the king of France and his wife were beheaded by the French radicals who had taken charge of the French Revolution. Name the ill-fated pair.

33 During the Industrial Revolution, the Luddites were manual laborers who took to extreme measures, including violence, to oppose the introduction of machinery, which they believed would put them out of work. For whom were the Luddites named?

34 The Bessemer Process, named in honor of Henry Bessemer (1813–98), gave quite a boost to the Industrial Revolution. What is the Bessemer Process?

35 In 1817 Bernardo O'Higgins was a leader of revolutionary forces that successfully wrested control of this country from a foreign power. What nation evolved from O'Higgins' efforts? (He became its first president.)

36 The first earl of Chatham, called "the Great Commoner," guided Britain's rise as the world's premier colonial power with possessions in Africa, India, and North America. By what name do we know the earl of Chatham?

37 In the English Civil War (1642–49) the adversaries were the Parliamentarians, known as the Roundheads, and the Royalists, who were followers of Charles I. Where did the Roundheads get their name?

38 For a brief period after the English Civil War (1649–60) Great Britain's monarchy was interrupted by a parliamentary government headed by a lord protector. Who was lord protector during this monarchical lapse?

39 In 1810 revolutionary fever spread to Mexico, which was under Spanish control, and was ruled by Joseph Napoleon, Bonaparte's brother. The unsuccessful series of revolts was first led by Miguel Hidalgo y Costilla and later by Jose Maria Morelos y Pavon. In addition to their quest for freedom, Hidalgo and Morelos shared the same profession. What was that profession?

40 The Great Hunger (1845–49) not only brought death to about one million people but also fueled a revolution. What was the Great Hunger?

41 The Industrial Revolution was helped along immeasurably by an invention of John Loudon McAdam (1756–1836). What was McAdam's contribution to forwarding the Revolution?

42 One of the most famous naval war heroes was Horatio Nelson (1758–1805), the British admiral who racked up an impressive series of naval victories in the eighteenth century. But Viscount Nelson suffered a loss in a battle at Calvi (1793) that stayed with him until his death in the Battle of Trafalgar. What was that loss?

43 President Joseph Roberts issued a Declaration of Independence in 1847. Of what fledgling nation was Roberts president?

44 One of London's major tourist attractions is Madame Tussaud's Wax Museum. Where did Madame Tussaud begin modeling her wax images of famous people?

45 Throughout the age of revolution, when much of the world was in a state of change, China was under the control of a single line of succession. The Ch'ing dynasty, the last of China's dynasties, ruled from 1644 to 1912, but this wasn't China's longest-reigning dynasty. Can you name the dynasty that was?

46 In 1688–89, William and Mary took over the throne of England, unseating James II. What was so unusual about this upheaval that it became known as the Glorious Revolution?

Answers

① *The rebel was François Dominique Toussaint L'Ouverture (1744–1803).*

② *The* ancien régime *was the rule of order in France until the French Revolution.*

③ *One of the major religions in the British colonies was that of the Anglican Communion—the Church of England. Following the colonial victory over Great Britain, a reorganization was necessary in the newborn United States. This resulted in the formation of the Protestant Episcopal Church.*

④ *The author of* Reflections on the French Revolution *is Edmund Burke (1729–97).*

⑤ *In 1822 Simón Bolívar founded El Gran Colombia, which later was divided into Colombia, Venezuela, and Ecuador.*

⑥ *Jacques Garnerin, a Frenchman, accomplished the feat in 1797.*

⑦ *Atahualpa was the last of the Inca Empire's rulers. Francisco Pizarro, a Spanish explorer/conquerer, had him put to death in 1533 after the Spanish defeated the Incas and won control of the Inca Empire.*

⑧ *The key to the Bastille hangs on the wall near the main staircase in Mount Vernon, George Washington's home in Virginia. It was presented to General Washington by the Marquis de Lafayette.*

⑨ *The Bastille was a medieval fortress that later became a state prison where political prisoners were incarcerated and often tortured.*

⑩ *He was a physician. (I don't think I'd want him operating on me.)*

⑪ *Haiti was the world's first black republic. Although its independence was* declared in 1804, France did not recognize that independence until twenty years later.

(12) *Robespierre was the leader of the Jacobins, whose name was derived from the convent of the Jacobin friars, where their founders' first meeting was held.*

(13) *The military action was precipitated by piracy. Brigands of Algiers, Tripoli, and Tunis were harassing U.S. merchant ships, so naval forces were dispatched to force the leaders of those nations to sign treaties to put an end to the practice.*

(14) *In 1811, some thirty years after the British surrender at Yorktown, Virginia, George III was declared insane, and his son, George, became regent of England. The son was crowned George IV following his father's death in 1820.*

(15) *1(c) Arkwright/the roller spinning frame (1769); 2(b) Cartwright/the power loom (1785); 3(e) Crompton/the spinning mule, or muslim wheel (1779); 4(d) Hargreave/the spinning jenny (1764); and 5(a) Kay/the flying shuttle (1733).*

(16) *After his act of treason against the colonial forces in the Revolution, General Benedict Arnold fought on the British side in the war.*

He emigrated to England following the British defeat, and years later left word of his desire to be buried in his American uniform.

⑰ *It was (d) William Pitt the Elder (1708–78) who said this in a speech before the British House of Commons on March 2, 1770. It should be noted that this was not in reference to the American Revolutionary War.*

⑱ *It's from the Latin ca-*put, *meaning "head," because usually the executions involved hanging or cutting off the heads of those sentenced to death.*

⑲ *Although at the time of his death he was viewed with much disdain, Simón Bolívar (1783–1830) is now immortalized for freeing Bolivia, Colombia, Ecuador, Peru, and Venezuela of foreign control.*

⑳ *It was the official method of execution in France until late in the twentieth century.*

㉑ *The Reign of Terror, sometimes called merely "The Terror," was the period in the French Revolution between June 1793 and July 1794 when the Jacobins, led by Maximilien Robespierre, took control of the Committee of Public Safety. Using threats of impending danger from invasions, they had thousands of royalists, priests, and foes of the*

Jacobins arrested, tried, and executed. In one six-week period, 1,285 were guillotined. Robespierre was eventually overthrown and executed.

(22) *Actually the name was not derived from the road; it came from the method of limiting access to the highways to those who paid their toll. The turnpike was the barricade, which was turned on its pike (or post) to allow those who paid the toll to enter the roadway.*

(23) *The French and Indian War was a carryover of the Seven Years' War between Prussia and Britain on one side, against a coalition of Austria, France, and Russia on the other.*

(24) *The legend says if the apes leave, the British will lose their piece of the Rock.*

(25) *In England and the United States, bushrangers were known as highwaymen—thieves who held up travelers.*

(26) *The Huguenots.*

(27) *Spain and Portugal held sway over most of South America.*

(28) *The Thirty-three Immortals helped in the creation of Uruguay, which had been part of Brazil.*

(29) *Aurangzeb, a Muslim, tried to force all of his subjects to convert to Islam, unleashing a revolt led by the Hindu princes.*

㉚ *Hung was a leader in the Taiping Rebellion (1850–64).*

㉛ *The war hero was Count Casimir Pulaski (1748–79).*

㉜ *It was Louis XVI and Marie Antoinette.*

㉝ *The original Luddites in 1811–16 England, were organized to attempt to destroy spinning and farm machinery, thinking these technological advances would cause massive unemployment. They were named for Ned Ludd (sometimes referred to as General Ludd or King Ludd), who some historians believe was a fictional character.*

㉞ *Bessemer, a British engineer, devised a method to remove carbon from molten iron, reducing the cost of steel production by close to eighty-five percent.*

㉟ *The name might be deceptive. O'Higgins' forces defeated the Spaniards at Chacabuco, and he became the first president of Chile. O'Higgins' father was the Irish-born viceroy of Chile and Peru.*

㊱ *The first earl of Chatham was William Pitt the Elder (1708–78), who was King George II's prime minister (1756–61).*

③⑦ *The Roundheads were so-called because of their short haircuts. The Royalists wore their hair long as was fashionable at that time.*

③⑧ *Oliver Cromwell was lord protector until his death in 1658. Cromwell's son, Richard, was then named lord protector. But in 1660 the government was overthrown by those dissatisfied with the Protectorate, and the monarchy was restored.*

③⑨ *Hidalgo and Morelos were both priests.*

④⓪ *The Great Hunger was a terrible famine that struck Ireland causing about a million Irish to emigrate to America. These emigrants founded the Fennian movement, an early attempt to sever Ireland from the British.*

④① *McAdam is the Scottish inventor of the macadam road surface, which vastly improved the speed of transporting goods and people. He proposed raising roads above the surrounding area for drainage, filling first with large rocks, followed by smaller stones and a gravel filler.*

④② *Nelson lost an eye during the battle at Calvi. He took advantage of this during the 1801 battle at Copenhagen, exercising his "right to be blind sometimes," he ignored a signal to break off the battle and ended up winning the day.*

43 *Roberts was the first president of Liberia, which was established on the west coast of Africa by the American Colonization Society in 1822 as a haven for slaves emigrating from the United States.*

44 *While imprisoned in France during the French Revolution, the Swiss-born Tussaud made models of the heads of famous persons who had been decapitated in the Reign of Terror.*

45 *The longest-reigning dynasty in China's history was the Chou Dynasty, which was in power from 1125 to 255* B.C.

46 *No blood was shed in the uprising; thus it was named the Glorious (or Bloodless) Revolution.*

A Century of Change

*F*ew people in history have had the impact of the pair who so influenced the world in the nineteenth century—Napoleon Bonaparte, with his dreams of conquest, and Queen Victoria, more for her longevity and her choices of prime minister. Their respective reigns wrought much change.

The questions in this chapter, however, will not be limited to their respective dominions. It was during this period that the effects of the Industrial Revolution really began to take hold, bringing sweeping changes in life styles, the methods of waging war, and the means and speed of transportation, both of goods and people. The period covered in this *chapter will take us up to the outbreak of World War I.*

❶ In 1831 Louis Philippe, the Citizen-King of France (1830–48), formed a unit termed the Regiments Etrangères. By what name do we know the *Regiments Etrangères*?

❷ The first earl of Beaconsfield won mild critical acclaim for his romantic novels, and some notoriety for his somewhat eccentric mode of dress. But history records many foreign policy achievements for which he is best remembered. Can you name this British prime minister?

❸ In 1812 Napoleon Bonaparte led between 500,000 and 700,000 soldiers in an ill-fated invasion of Russia. The majority of the French emperor's troops on this mission were not French. What nationality were they?

❹ Relative to the preceding question, name the Russian czar who in 1812 thwarted Napoleon's invasion of Russia, then marched victoriously into Paris two years later.

❺ The reign of Queen Victoria made an almost immeasurable mark on the world both during and following her years on the throne of Great Britain. How many years did Victoria reign?

6 Here's a "Who Said It?" question for you. "Let China sleep. When she awakens the world will be sorry." Who Said It: (a) Napoleon Bonaparte, (b) Winston Churchill, (c) Benjamin Disraeli, or (d) Karl Marx?

7 One of the most coveted international awards is the Nobel Prize. Here's a multipart question for you. (a) For whom are the Nobel Prizes named, (b) in what year were they first awarded, and (c) in what five categories were they originally awarded?

8 The Nobel Prizes are presented in two countries—Norway and Sweden. Why are they given in two separate countries?

9 In 1859 Charles Darwin's book, explaining what has come down to us as "Darwin's Theory of Evolution," was published. What did Darwin cite as the basic factor in evolution? For extra credit, care to take a stab at the twenty-two word title of Darwin's book?

10 There are some interesting sidelights to Charles Darwin that are totally unrelated to his "Theory of Evolution." Let's look at just two: (a) Darwin's mother, Susannah Wedgwood, came from a family whose name is well-known to this day. Why? And (b) Charles Darwin was born on February 12, 1809, the exact day as another historic person. Name the man who was born on the same day as Darwin.

11 Name the nineteenth-century French chemist who developed a vaccine against rabies.

12 Father Joseph Mohr was the vicar of Saint Nicholas Church in Oberndorf, Austria. What was Father Joseph's contribution to Christmas celebrations?

13 An aircraft, named the *Gyroplane*, lifted off at Douai, France, on September 19, 1907. What makes this brief flight so historic?

14 The Arc de Triomphe, weakened by traffic and sinking foundations, is currently being restored. Who ordered the original construction (1806–36) of this monument to French military victories?

15 Who is entombed in the Arc de Triomphe?

16 The first nation to adopt a general income tax did so in 1799. Can you guess what country initiated this type of levy?

17 In the eighteenth and nineteenth centuries, Dutch settlers in southern Africa established what is known as *baasskap*, or boss-hood. What is boss-hood?

18 The awarding of Olympic medals was instituted when the games were revived in 1896, but only first- and second-place winners were so honored. As you probably know, today's victors receive gold for first place, silver for second, and bronze for third. Which two of these did the first- and second-place winners in 1896 receive?

19 On the subject of the revival of the Olympics, in what city were the 1896 games held? (Hint: A little thought makes this an easy question.)

20 Who was known as the "Lady with the Lamp"?

21 Each year millions of dollars are raised for charity through the sale of Christmas seals. In what country was this idea first put forward by a postal clerk?

22 We won't ask what the first four were, but can you name what Napoleon Bonaparte once referred to as "the fifth element" of war?

23 When Victoria succeeded her uncle, William IV, and became queen of Great Britain, the Salic Laws prevented her from also succeeding to the Hanoverian throne. What were the Salic Laws?

24 In their first appearance in the modern Olympics, women were confined to diving and swimming. In what year was that?

25 In 1912 China became a republic. Who was the first president of the Chinese Republic?

26 In any look at the naval history of the world it's hard to bypass the accomplishments of a pair of Americans—the Perry brothers, Matthew and Oliver. One played a key role in opening Japan to U.S. trade. The other was the hero against the British ships in the Battle of Lake Erie in the War of 1812. Which brother played which role?

27 October 10 is celebrated as "Double Ten" day by people of what nationality?

28 What country can lay claim to having the first railway in the world to use steam locomotives?

29 May 1—May Day— was very important in the Communist-dominated countries. Where did the custom of May Day as a day of celebration originate?

30 Here's a "Name Him" question. This federal judge was the first governor-general of the Philippines (1901). He later became president of the United States. Name him.

31 Here's a two-part question for you. On December 11, 1901, Guglielmo Marconi sent the first transatlantic radio signal. Here are the questions: (a) What was the message, and (b) between what two points was the message sent?

32 The fall of Russia's Czar Nicholas was in no small measure due to the spiritual influence the "Mad Monk" had over Czarina Alexandra. Who was the Mad Monk? And how did he come to have such control over Alexandra?

33 What two men are considered the founders of the Socialist-Communist movement?

34 Name the book, coauthored by the two founders of the Socialist-Communist movement, on which much of Communist theory is based.

35 The most coveted decoration for gallantry among the British is the Victoria Cross. In what war was this citation first bestowed?

36 London's rapid transit system, the world's oldest electric system (1890), is not called a subway. What do Londoners call their system?

37 Few poems are better known than Alfred, Lord Tennyson's *Charge of the Light Brigade*. In what war did the battle occur that inspired Tennyson's immortal piece?

38 You don't read much about the Boer War in South Africa (1899–1902), but at least four "firsts" are attributed to that conflict. Can you name any one of these?

39 In 1990 Lech Walesa, who was so prominent in the drive to free Poland from Communist rule, was presented with a special award in a ceremony that took place in the oldest continually operating theater in the United States. Can you name this historic theater, which opened its doors in 1809?

40 Although we automatically think of the United States whenever we hear of the Panama Canal, in reality, work on the canal was taken over by the United States when the original project went bankrupt. What nation started work on the waterway?

41 Who led the respective forces in the Battle of Waterloo (June 1815)?

42 Where is Waterloo?

43 Lola Montez, the legendary nineteenth-century dancer, gained notoriety as the mistress of King Louis I of Bavaria. What nationality was the exotic dancer who was made a countess and later exiled, only to die in poverty?

44 The famed statue known as the Christ of the Andes, which was officially dedicated in 1904, was erected to commemorate the peace and boundary treaties between which two South American countries?

45 Name the nation, and for extra credit the year, in which the Christmas card originated.

46 What modern-day nation stands on the site that earned the nickname "Cockpit of Europe" by being the site of more battles between warring nations than any other European country?

47 Who was the first president of the United States to travel to a foreign nation while he was in office?

48 Which nineteenth-century president is the only U.S. chief executive to have had a foreign capital named in his honor? Name the country.

49 What inspired the coining of the term "yellow journalism"?

50 Name the three main foreign possessions won by the United States as a result of the Spanish-American War.

51 Cecil Rhodes (1853–1902) gained fame and fortune and wrote his name in South African history. This British statesman co-founded the famed De Beers diamond producing firm, gave his name to Rhodesia (albeit not permanently), and endowed the Rhodes Scholarships. What sent Rhodes to South Africa?

52 Name the woman who became queen-empress of India in May 1876.

53 The rebellion against British authorities in India by Hindu and Muslim soldiers, who were called *sepoys*, on May 10, 1857, which became known as the Sepoy Mutiny, was precipitated by the introduction of new rifle cartridges. What process involving these cartridges provoked the violent outburst?

54 The Sepoy Mutiny wrought a major change in Britain's administration in India. Can you name that administrative change?

55 Few inventions have had as much effect on civilization as has the automobile. Where was the first internal combustion engine used to operate a vehicle?

56 The Suez Canal, which was built between 1859 and 1869, was of untold importance to world trade. Here's a two-part question on this important waterway. (a) Who built the canal, and (b) what two bodies of water does the canal link?

57 The Berlin Conference (1884–85) had a lasting effect on the world. What was the main purpose of the Berlin Conference?

58 The Swedish chemist who invented dynamite in 1867 is world famous, but not only for this invention. Who was he?

59 Among the policies instituted during his term as chancellor (1871–90) were that of "blood and guts" and Kulturkampf, which was intended to subjugate the Catholic church to the government. Who was this German leader?

60 Over 500 people were killed in 1905 in what has come to be called Bloody Sunday. What revolution was launched by Bloody Sunday? And, what were the demands made by the demonstrators in this encounter?

61 From 1899 to 1902, an ongoing conflict between Dutch settlers in southern Africa and the British broke out in war. What was the name of that war?

62 "Religion . . . is the opium of the people." Who Said It: (a) Benjamin Disraeli, (b) Sigmund Freud, (c) Nikolai Lenin, or (d) Karl Marx?

63 Panama was not the first choice of the First Isthmian Canal Commission as a site for a waterway to connect the Atlantic and Pacific Oceans. What Central American country was their first choice?

64 In 1852 Henri Giffard, a French engineer, introduced his invention, which was powered by a three horsepower engine. What was Giffard's innovation?

65 When we think of the African slave trade it is almost automatically linked to the use of slaves on American plantations. But there was another heavy use of African slaves in the nineteenth century. In what commerce was that?

66 Practically everyone has heard the story of Sir Henry Stanley's search in Africa for David Livingstone in 1871, which culminates with the famed, "Dr. Livingstone, I presume?" But do you know what Livingstone was doing in Africa?

67 While we're on the subject of Sir Henry Stanley, here's an interesting question on his colorful career. Stanley once fought in a war on both sides. In what war was this?

68 The life of Napoleon Bonaparte began and ended on islands. He was born on an island, exiled to a second, and finally, after an attempted comeback, exiled to a third where he died. Name the three islands of importance in Napoleon's life.

69 The Russians suffered an embarrassing defeat in the Russo-Japanese War (1904–05). What caused that conflict?

70 The novels produced by the pen of this nineteenth-century British author are virtual treatises advocating social reforms. You've probably read him, but can you name this court stenographer turned novelist?

71 An innovation made at the Geneva Convention of 1864 has had an important effect on battlefield casualties. What was instituted at that conference?

72 Name the Norwegian who made the first transit of the Northwest Passage (1903–04) and was the first person to reach the South Pole (1911).

73 Sir George Cayley's 1852 invention set the pace for future generations and fulfilled dreams of inventors dating back to

Roger Bacon and Leonardo da Vinci. What did the British scientist invent?

74 Leon Trotsky (1879–1940), who would go on to prominence as a cofounder of the Soviet Union, was born Lev Davidovich Bronstein. How did he become known as Leon Trotsky?

75 China was the scene of a conflict in 1900 that wrought much change in Asia. By what name does history describe the conflict?

76 Originally named *The Leviathan, The Great Eastern*, a mammoth ship driven by a combination of paddle, screw, and sails, was a failure as a passenger ship. The ship, however, made history for another of its accomplishments (1865–73). What was this service?

Answers

① *The Regiments Etrangères is the Foreign Legion. The Legion was originally comprised of seven battalions, each manned by warriors of a single nationality.*

② *The eccentric earl of Beaconsfield is more widely known as Benjamin Disraeli (1804–81).*

③ *Less than one-third were French. The rest were from nations "liberated" by Napoleon: Germany, Austria, Italy, and Poland.*

④ *The Russian leader was Czar Alexander I, who ruled from 1801 to 1825.*

⑤ *Victoria was queen of England for sixty-four years (1837–1901).*

⑥ *(a) This warning came from Napoleon Bonaparte.*

⑦ *(a) Named for Swedish chemist-engineer Alfred Bernhard Nobel, (b) the prizes were first distributed on the fifth anniversary of his death: December 10, 1901, (c) in the categories of Chemistry, Literature, Peace, Physiology (or Medicine), and Physics.*

⑧ *In 1895, when Swedish chemist Alfred Nobel wrote his will establishing the awards, Norway and Sweden were politically united.*

⑨ *Darwin's Theory espoused natural selection as the basic factor in evolution. According to the theory, those organisms better adapted to the environment have a better chance of surviving than those that are not environmentally adaptable. As for the title, here goes:* On the Origin of the Species by Means of Natural Selection or the Preservation of Favoured Races in the Struggle for Life.

⑩ *(a) Wedgwood is perhaps the most famous name in the pottery field. We're sure you have heard of Wedgwood china. (b) On the day Darwin was born in Shrewsbury, England, Abraham Lincoln was drawing his first breath in rural Kentucky.*

⑪ *In addition to discovering the process named in his honor (pasteurization), Louis Pasteur (1822–95) developed a vaccine against rabies.*

⑫ *On Christmas Eve, 1818, Father Mohr wrote a poem, which was set to music by Franz Gruber, a schoolteacher and church organist in neighboring Arnsdorf. The resultant song was the lovely carol,* Silent Night, Holy Night, *or, as the Austrians say,* Stille Nacht, Heilige Nacht.

⑬ *The liftoff to a height just two feet off the ground was the first manned helicopter flight. The craft had four biplane rotors.*

⑭ *In 1806 Napoleon Bonaparte gave the order for the Arc de Triomphe's construction. Naturally, this was before he met his Waterloo.*

⑮ *The Arc is the site of the Tomb of France's Unknown Soldier.*

⑯ *The income tax was hatched in Great Britain. (H-m-m-m-m! Seems the American colonies cleared out at the right time.)*

⑰ *Boss-hood, which is white domination, was the forerunner to apartheid.*

⑱ *There were no gold medals awarded in 1896; first-place winners received silver; second-place winners bronze.*

⑲ *The Olympics were revived in Athens, Greece, in tribute to the ancient games.*

⑳ *Florence Nightingale (1820–1910), considered the founder of modern nursing, was the "Lady with the Lamp," a title she earned by working night and day in her battlefield hospital wards.*

㉑ *It was instituted in 1903 by Einar Holboll, a postal clerk in Denmark.*

㉒ *Napoleon called "mud" the fifth element of war.*

㉓ *Salic Laws forbade women from succeeding to titles in certain countries.*

㉔ *The Olympics were revived in 1896, but women were not included in the games until 1912.*

㉕ *The first president of China was Sun Yat-sen (1866–1925).*

㉖ *Commodore Matthew Perry (1794–1858) led the force that opened Japan to trade in 1853–54. His brother, Oliver Hazard Perry (1785–1819), commanded the fleet that defeated the British flotilla on Lake Erie (1813), sending home the message, "We have met the enemy, and they are ours." Quite a family.*

㉗ *The Chinese celebrate Double Ten as the anniversary of the successful revolt against Manchu rulers led by Sun Yet-sen in 1911.*

㉘ *Stockton and Darlington, which opened in England in 1825, was the first rail system in the world to use steam locomotives.*

㉙ *Though no one really knows, the festivities are widely believed to have originated as sort of a rite of spring. The Communists' celebration dates back to 1889 when the Second Socialist International declared May Day as a holiday for radicals.*

㉚ *On July 4, 1901, President William McKinley appointed William Howard Taft to the post of civil governor of the Philippines.*

㉛ *(a) The message was the Morse Code signal for the letter S, which was transmitted (b) from Cornwall, England, to Saint John's Newfoundland.*

㉜ *The Mad Monk was Grigori Yefimovich Rasputin, who was assassinated in 1916. Rasputin won influence over Alexandra be-*

cause he was able to ease the pain of Nicholas and Alexandra's hemophiliac son, Alexis.

(33) *The two founders are Friedrich Engels (1820–1895) and Karl Marx (1818–1883).*

(34) *It's the* Communist Manifesto, *written in 1848.*

(35) *The Victoria Cross was first awarded in the Crimean War (1853–56); the war pitted Russia against Turkey, Britain, France, and Sardinia.*

(36) *The "Underground" is referred to by Londoners as the "Tubes."*

(37) *It was in the Battle of Balaclava, which occurred on October 25, 1854, during the Crimean War.*

(38) *Take your pick. The Boer War saw the first use of motorcycles in combat, the first use of motorized trucks, the first use of radios in naval war, and the first time battle scenes were filmed on motion pictures.*

(39) *Walesa was awarded the Philadelphia Liberty Medal in the Walnut Street Theater in the City of Brotherly Love.*

(40) *The Panama Canal project was begun by a French company in 1881, but*

was abandoned in 1889 when the company went bankrupt.

④ *The French troops, led by Napoleon Bonaparte (Napoleon I), were defeated by British and Prussian forces under the command of Arthur Wellesley, first duke of Wellington, and Gebhard Leberecht von Blucher.*

④ *It's in South Belgium.*

④ *Her pseudonym doesn't sound it, but Lola Montez (real name: Gilbert) was Irish.*

④ *The Christ of the Andes was dedicated in 1904 to mark the pacts between Argentina and Chile.*

④ *British artist John Calcott Horsley created the first card for a wealthy client, Sir Henry Cole, to send to his friends in 1843.*

④ *Belgium was given the nickname "Cockpit of Europe."*

④ *Teddy Roosevelt, the nation's twenty-sixth president, cruised to Panama on the U.S.S. Louisiana in 1906.*

④ *Monrovia, the capital of Liberia, was named in honor of James Monroe.*

④ *The term was first used in 1898 to describe the sensationalism employed by*

William Randolph Hearst's New York Journal *and Joseph Pulitzer's* New York World *in reporting alleged Spanish atrocities in Cuba. The papers were rapt in competition for readership in Gotham.*

50 *The Treaty of Paris (December 10, 1898) ceded control of Guam, the Philippines, and Puerto Rico to the United States. Cuba also gained its independence from Spain from the treaty.*

51 *On two occasions, severe illness struck Rhodes, and on both incidents, he went to South Africa to recuperate. His investment in diamond mines there resulted in his amassing a fortune.*

52 *Prime Minister Benjamin Disraeli arranged to have this title bestowed on Queen Victoria.*

53 *The cartridges were to be greased with cow and pig fat, which was counter to the religious beliefs of the* sepoys.

54 *The widespread revolt by the* sepoys *resulted in the transfer of administrative control in India from the British East India Company to the British crown.*

55 *In 1885 Karl Benz used an internal combustion engine in a forerunner to the modern automobile in Germany. In that same year,*

Gottlieb Daimler came out with a much-improved version.

56 *The Suez Canal, (a) constructed by a private French company, (b) links the Mediterranean Sea and the Red Sea.*

57 *The Berlin Conference, in effect, dealt with the claims of European nations on lands in Africa, chiefly the Belgians' claims on the Congo.*

58 *The man who invented dynamite also bequeathed the famed annual awards we know as the Nobel prizes, Alfred Bernhard Nobel.*

59 *The German chancellor (1871–90) was Otto von Bismarck.*

60 *Bloody Sunday touched off the Russian Revolution of 1905. The workers, led by Father Gapon, a priest, marched on the palace in Saint Petersburg demanding an eight-hour workday, a one-ruble-per-day minimum wage, and a constituent assembly.*

61 *It was the Boer War, which derived its name from the Dutch word for farmer. The conflict dated back to an earlier declaration abolishing slavery throughout the British empires.*

62 *(d) Karl Marx (1818–83) wrote this in the* Critique of the Hegelian Philosophy of Right *(1844).*

(63) *The commission favored a passageway through Nicaragua.*

(64) *Giffard's invention was the first successful dirigible, a cigar-shaped, lighter-than-air craft, which flew at a speed of six miles per hour.*

(65) *Many African natives were bought by Arab slave traders to be sold to those who were transporting elephant tusks through Africa.*

(66) *Livingstone was in Africa as a medical missionary, who also did some exploring, which resulted in the discovery of Victoria Falls.*

(67) *As a fifteen-year-old cabin boy on a cruise from Wales to New Orleans, Stanley jumped ship. A few years later when the Civil War broke out, he joined the "Dixie Grays," a Confederate unit. Following his capture at Shiloh, Stanley accepted an offer to swear allegiance to the Union and joined the Northern army. His combat experience was quite brief.*

(68) *Born of Italian heritage on the island of Corsica in 1769 (the very year Corsica became a French possession), Napoleon was exiled on the island of Elba (1814), then after a failed comeback, exiled again to the island of Saint Helena where he died (1821).*

⑥⑨ The Russo-Japanese War was brought on by rival claims over control of Manchuria and Korea. Following the Treaty of Portsmouth, all Russia retained was control over northern Manchuria.

⑦⓪ It is the creator of such immortal characters as David Copperfield, Uriah Heep, Tiny Tim, and Ebenezer Scrooge—Charles Dickens (1812–70).

⑦① It was agreed at that convention that with some conditions, hospital and ambulance staffs were declared neutral in combat situations.

⑦② The explorer was Roald Amundsen (1872–1928). He died while searching for the Italian airship Italia, which was lost on a polar flight.

⑦③ Cayley produced the first glider capable of carrying a human passenger.

⑦④ In 1902 Bronstein was exiled to Siberia for his revolutionary activities. He escaped in 1902 with the aid of a passport stolen from one of his jailers, whose name was Trotsky. He kept the name.

⑦⑤ It was the Boxer Rebellion, an outbreak of violence aimed at ridding China of foreigners and those Chinese who had strong incli-

nations toward Western influence. The group leading the fray called itself the Fists of Righteous Harmony.

⑦⑥ The Great Eastern *was the craft used to lay the transatlantic cables for the transmission of telegraph messages.*

World War I and Internationalism

Many historians refer to the U.S. Civil War as the first modern war, because it was the first to use many of the advances in technology, but it did not match the losses in World War I. World War I was the first war to involve so many nations. True, there were earlier wars in which more than two nations were engaged, but the scale of World War I was unequaled. On the Allied side, you had such nations as the United States, Great Britain, France, and Russia. And across the line of battle were the Central Powers, including Germany, Austro-Hungary, and Turkey.

It was the first war in which aircraft played a major role, and naval vessels *were powered by engines rather than sails. High-powered weaponry had a much wider range of destruction. Here we had a tragic example of the dangers that can accompany the benefits of modern inventions.*

There were, however, also bright spots in the era we're about to enter on our journey through the Who, What, When, Where, Why in the World of World History. *With the "shrinking" of the world thanks to speedier methods of travel, more people were able to extend their horizons. Immigration was made easier, as were international communications. Let's look at the World War I era.*

❶ World War I was the ultimate outgrowth of a chain reaction starting with an assassination that took place in Sarajevo, Yugoslavia. Who was the victim of this assassination?

2 What country was the first to declare war in the sequence of events leading ultimately to World War I?

3 The Triple Entente was formed in the days preceding World War I to counter the Triple Alliance. Can you name the nations that constituted each of these?

4 One of America's most beloved WWI flying aces was Captain Eddie Rickenbacker (1890–1973). In his autobiography, Rickenbacker said he emulated a pilot who died in that conflict while a member of the Lafayette Escadrille. Can you name the man Rickenbacker called "the greatest pilot of them all . . . the American Ace of Aces"?

5 Speaking of WWI and the Lafayette Escadrille, another flying ace in that unit, James Hall, went on after the war to coauthor a classic novel that was based on an historic event. Can you name the book coauthored by Hall and Charles Nordhoff? (Hint: It was recreated on film three times.)

6 One of the earliest examples of terrorists sending bombs through the mail occurred during World War I. A radical labor group—the Industrial Workers of the World (IWW), which was opposed to U.S. entry into the war—was suspected of mailing bombs to eighteen Americans they viewed as being antiunion. By what other name were members of the IWW known?

7 Those early-1900 mail bombs all failed for the same reason. Can you cite the reason for their fortunate failure?

8 Veterans' Day was originally designated as Armistice Day to mark the end of World War I. The Armistice occurred on the eleventh day of the eleventh month—November 11. Your question? In what year did this take place?

9 Turkey was among the nations fighting on the German side against the Allied forces in World War I. Can you name the man who became famous in the postwar era for stirring Arab forces against the Turks? Avid movie-goers will know this one.

10 Until the 1910s, Christmas card sales in the United States were dominated by imported cards. What reversed this, and what country had formerly produced the bulk of those imported greeting cards?

11 One of the most infamous tragedies in World War I was the sinking of the *Lusitania*. What was the national origin of the liner?

12 As a follow-up to the preceding question, how many people were killed when the *Lusitania* was sunk?

13 Soviet Russia received a setback in its international relations because of the Treaty of Brest-Litovsk. What was this treaty?

14 In 1919 the Comintern was established. What was the Comintern?

15 One of the phrases created by the Germans in World War I was reference to the Devil Dogs. To what/whom were they referring?

16 In the late nineteenth century, every major European nation, except one, instituted a policy of building armies by conscription. Name the only country that shunned this practice of universal drafts.

17 The Lafayette Escadrille consisted of Americans who joined in the fight against Germany prior to the United States' entry into World War I. Where was the Lafayette Escadrille based?

18 The Balfour Declaration, issued in November 1917 by British Foreign Secretary Arthur Balfour, has had a deep and lasting impact over the decades in the Middle East. What was the main point of controversy in this declaration?

19 President Woodrow Wilson's strong reaction to the Germans' sinking of the *Lusitania* with his demands for an apology so upset his secretary of state that the cabinet member resigned. Who was that secretary of state?

20 Japan was allied with Nazi Germany in World War II. Did Japan take sides in the First World War?

21 During the drive to force the Germans back across the Marne River (September 5–14, 1914), the French military governor of Paris used 1,200 vehicles to carry reinforcements to the front. What type of vehicles were used in this effort?

22 A French-born physician living in the United States, Dr. Alexis Carrel, performed the first successful heart surgery in 1914. What was unusual about the patient?

23 In the early days of the Communist takeover of Russia, there were two branches of Marxist socialism that grew into the Soviet Empire. Name the two factions, and tell which won out.

24 A ploy used by the British to deceive German vessels to keep them from assaulting British merchant ships caused a stir in World War I. What was the method of deception?

㉕ Who were the Anzacs?

㉖ Name the emperor who ruled Germany during World War I.

㉗ The League to Enforce Peace was organized in Philadelphia's Independence Hall in an effort to end the war in 1915. Who was the president of the league?

㉘ The words czar and kaiser had a common heritage. What was it?

㉙ A medicine, which had been sold by prescription since 1897, was finally made available in tablet form in 1915 by a German pharmaceutical firm. What was this medicine?

㉚ One of the most popular tunes of the World War I era was *Pack Up Your Troubles in Your Old Kit Bag*. What is a kit bag?

㉛ In the days prior to the U.S. entry into World War I, a U.S. military expedition crossed the border into Mexico to apprehend a Mexican rebel who was wreaking havoc in the Southwest. Name the general who led that expedition, and the rebel he sought (unsuccessfully) to apprehend.

㉜ November 7 marks the anniversary of an event that took place in 1917 which has had a lasting effect on the world. What was that disastrous occurrence?

33 What land was purchased by the United States from Denmark in 1916?

34 An innovation in World War I was the British Army's *Little Willie*. What was the Little Willie?

35 Vladimir Ilich Ulyanov's dreams of seeing his ideology spread throughout the world are crumbling in East Europe. Who was this Communist party founder?

36 During World War I U.S. infantrymen were often referred to as doughboys. Where did that nickname originate?

37 The kingdom of the Serbs, Croats, and Slovenes was established in 1918. By what name do we know this country?

38 Prior to U.S. entry into World War I, the Germans made an offer to the government of Mexico to lure them into joining the German war effort. What did the Germans offer Mexico?

39 Who ruled Russia in the period between the fall of the czarist government and the takeover by the Bolsheviks?

40 Here's a "Who Said It?" question. "The world must be made safe for democracy." Who said it, and in what important speech?

41 In 1917 Britain's King George V changed his family name to Windsor. Why?

42 One of the civilian casualties of World War I was a Dutch woman, Margaretha Zelle, who was executed by the French. By what name might you know Zelle?

43 Under what command did the first Americans enter the front lines in World War I?

44 When U.S. forces arrived in France to join the war against the Germans, a U.S. Army officer delivered the following message at the gravesite of the Marquis de Lafayette: "Lafayette, nous voila," translation, "Lafayette, we are here." Who said it?

45 How did the Communists come to be called "Reds"?

46 In 1918, to ease the friction caused by having different commanders, the Americans, British, French, and Italians combined their forces under a single commander-in-chief. Who received this appointment?

47 One of the most honored U.S. units in World War I is the 42nd Division, which became known as the Rainbow Division. How did it get this nickname?

48 The commander of the Rainbow Division went on to become one of history's most revered military leaders. Name him.

49 Early in 1918 President Wilson presented his *Fourteen Points* to Congress, which contained one calling for "a general association of nations," a forecast of a League of Nations. Here's a "Who Said It?" question for you. "President Wilson and his Fourteen Points bore me. Even God Almighty had only ten." Was it (a) Winston Churchill, (b) Georges Clemenceau, or (c) Henry Cabot Lodge?

50 Saint Petersburg was the capital of Russia (later the Soviet Union) from 1712 until 1922. It underwent two name changes before the name Saint Petersburg was restored in 1991. What two names did the city bear under Soviet control?

51 The long-range artillery weapons used by the Germans to shell Paris (some seventy-five miles away) were called "Big Berthas." Where did they get this name?

52 Czar Nicholas, Czarina Alexandra, and their five children were executed by the Communists in 1918. But through the following decades, legends grew claiming one child had survived the brutal slaying of the family. What was the name of the reputed survivor?

53 In 1918–19 twenty million people around the world died, but not from the war. What was the cause of this massive loss of lives?

54 The armistice ending World War I was signed at 5 A.M. on November 11, 1918. In what type of building was the peace agreement inked?

55 When President Woodrow Wilson headed the U.S. delegation to the Peace Conference in Versailles he made a major diplomatic blunder regarding the composition of the delegation. What was this mistake?

56 Germany's fixation on having "a place in the sun" is seen as one of the reasons for both World Wars. Who coined this phrase?

57 What country evolved from the 1916 Easter Uprising, a demonstration involving some two thousand people?

58 Lieutenant Colonel John McCrae, a Canadian medical officer serving in France, wrote one of history's most famous poems while serving in World War I. Can you name it?

Answers

① *The victim was Archduke Francis Ferdinand, heir apparent to the throne of Austro-Hungary, who was murdered along with his wife on June 28, 1914.*

② *Austro-Hungary declared war on Serbia. Archduke Ferdinand's assassin was a Serbian.*

③ *In 1907 France, Great Britain, and Russia formed the Triple Entente to counter the threat of the Triple Alliance comprised of Austria-Hungary, Germany, and Italy, which dated to 1882.*

④ *Rickenbacker's model was the third-ranking American air ace, Raoul Lufbery of the famed Lafayette Escadrille. Lufbery jumped from his burning plane when it plunged to the earth over France, and was impaled on a picket fence.*

⑤ *The World War I flying ace coauthored* Mutiny on the Bounty.

⑥ *The* IWW *members were known as the Wobblies.*

⑦ *The packages did not carry sufficient postage.*

⑧ *In 1918.*

⑨ *You'd know him by the name of his film biography, which, in 1962, won the Oscar for movie of the year,* Lawrence of Arabia. *It was Thomas E. Lawrence (1888–1935), who organized the Arabs in a revolt against the Turks in World War I.*

⑩ *World War I brought an embargo on German imports, which was the major source of Christmas cards for the United States. The man credited with establishing the Christmas card as a tradition in the United States was Louis Prang, a German who emigrated to Boston in 1850.*

⑪ *The* Lusitania, *which was sunk by a German submarine off the Irish coast on May 7, 1915, was flying the British flag.*

⑫ *The sinking of the British liner resulted in 1,195 deaths, of which 128 were Americans.*

⑬ *The Treaty of Brest-Litovsk, signed March 3, 1918, was a separate treaty between the Soviets and the Central Powers (Germany, Austria-Hungary, Bulgaria, and the Ottoman Empire) to end World War I. This unilateral act by the Soviets angered the Allied nations.*

⑭ *Founded by Vladimir Lenin to coordinate control over Communist groups around the globe, the Comintern was an acronym for*

Communist International, or the Third International.

⑮ The Devil Dogs are better known as the United States Marines, who played a key part in dogging the Germans into submission.

⑯ Great Britain was the only major European nation that did not have compulsory military service in that period.

⑰ The name should have given it away. The Lafayette Escadrille operated as part of the French Aviation Service.

⑱ The Balfour Declaration said, "His Majesty's Government view (sic) with favor the establishment in Palestine of a national home for the Jewish people . . ." In effect, this endorsed the State of Israel.

⑲ It was Secretary of State William Jennings Bryan.

⑳ The Japanese were on the Allied side in World War I, declaring war on Germany in 1914.

㉑ The reinforcements were carried by taxicabs. (Could that be why some cabbies drive like they're in battlefront conditions?)

㉒ The patient was a dog.

㉓ The Menshevik branch was absorbed, or liquidated, by the Bolshevik faction.

(24) *President Woodrow Wilson strongly protested the British act of flying U.S. flags on its merchant ships.*

(25) *The Anzacs were the combined Australian and New Zealand Army Corps.*

(26) *Kaiser Wilhelm II.*

(27) *The league was presided over by former U.S. President William Howard Taft.*

(28) *Both words came from the Latin word—caesar.*

(29) *It was aspirin, released by the Bayer company.*

(30) *A kit bag is well-known to those in the military, but they refer to it as a knapsack, which is the more accepted name for it.*

(31) *General John J. Pershing led 6,000 men in an effort to capture Francisco Pancho Villa in 1916. Villa had been wreaking havoc on U.S. citizens and border towns because President Woodrow Wilson had recognized Villa's opponent in the Mexican revolution.*

(32) *The October Revolution of 1917, which put the Bolsheviks in control of Russia, is celebrated by the Communist regime on November 7. It actually occurred in October, but that was under the old-style calendar.*

③③ *The land was the Virgin Islands, which became U.S. property on January 1, 1917.*

③④ *It was a tank.*

③⑤ *This follower of Marxism is better known by his adopted name Vladimir Ilich Lenin (1870–1924).*

③⑥ *It is believed to have been coined in reference to the dumpling-like buttons worn on infantry uniforms in the Civil War*

③⑦ *In 1929 the kingdom of Serbs, Croats, and Slovenes became Yugoslavia.*

③⑧ *They offered the Mexicans the U.S. states of Arizona, New Mexico, and Texas.*

③⑨ *The provisional government, which was overthrown in the October 1917 Bolshevik Revolution, was headed first by Prince Lvov, then by Alexander Kerensky. Lvov and Kerensky had been appointed by the Russian Duma (parliament) to head the government after the czar was dethroned.*

④⓪ *The phrase was in President Woodrow Wilson's April 2, 1917, address before a special session of Congress calling for a declaration of war against Germany.*

④① *George V wanted to sever all ties with his family's German ancestry. So* the family name was changed from Saxe-Coburg-Gotha to Windsor.

(42) Zelle was the exotic dancer convicted of spying for the Germans. We know her by her stage name—Mata Hari.

(43) The first U.S. troops in combat were under French command.

(44) While many attribute the statement to General John Pershing, Pershing said the phrase was coined by Colonel Charles E. Stanton (1859–1933). Stanton was referring to the United States' returning the favor of Lafayette's participation in the American Revolution.

(45) It was from the color of their flag during the Bolshevik Revolution. Red flags had also been carried by revolutionary socialists in the nineteenth century.

(46) The commander in chief was Marshal Ferdinand Foch of the French army.

(47) It was called the Rainbow Division because it was composed of National Guard units from a wide range of states.

(48) The Rainbow Division's chief of staff was Colonel Douglas MacArthur.

(49) *(b) French Premier Clemenceau apparently was turned off by Wilson's rhetorical call for a world body.*

(50) *The Soviets changed Saint Petersburg's name to Petrograd in 1914, then Leningrad in 1924.*

(51) *The Big Berthas were named after Bertha von Krupp, proprietress of the Krupp Munitions Works where they were manufactured.*

(52) *Anastasia was the daughter immortalized in text and film as having survived the execution.*

(53) *The lives were lost due to an influenza epidemic. In the United States alone twenty million people were stricken, and of these some 850,000 died.*

(54) *The armistice was signed in a railroad car in Compiegne forest, north of Paris.*

(55) *Wilson, a Democrat, did not include any members of the Republican-controlled Senate in the delegation.*

(56) *The expression is attributed to Count Bernhard von Bulow, who was the German chancellor from 1900 to 1909.*

⑤⑦ *The Easter Uprising in Dublin led to the creation three years later of the Sinn Fein party, which established an independent Irish Parliament. Britain eventually was forced to recognize the Irish Free State (1922), which in turn led to the independent Republic of Ireland (1949).*

⑤⑧ *McCrae is the author of the poignant work* In Flanders Fields. *He died in France on January 28, 1918, after having served four years on the Western Front.*

A Lull Between
the Storms

With the close of World War I—the war to end all wars—the nations of the world went about the task of rebuilding and reviving their domestic affairs, but they would only have about two decades before the next outburst by a would-be world conqueror.

The years between the storms would see many changes—socially, economically, and internationally. Depressions, international crime, new dance crazes, national takeovers, inventions galore, all were squeezed into this lull between the storms.

1 The League of Nations was established in 1920. In what year was it dissolved?

2 What was the intent of the 1928 Kellogg-Briand Treaty, named in honor of U.S. Secretary of State Frank Kellogg and French Foreign Minister Aristide Briand?

3 For several decades, the ruling party of the Republic of China (Taiwan) has been the Kuomintang, which was originally formed in 1912. Why should this not be referred to as "the Kuomintang party"?

4 In the 1936 Berlin Summer Olympics, a black U.S. athlete embarrassed Adolf Hitler by running off (pun intended) with four gold medals in track and field. Who was this immortal athlete?

5 Eric Arthur Blair (1903–50) was one of England's most famous writers. His works are often cited by communism's foes. What was Blair's pen name?

6 You've probably heard of the Rastafarians, a Jamaican cult, but do you know the origin of the name of the sect? (Hint: It's the original name of an African leader, who later changed his name.)

7 In what year were the first Winter Olympics held?

8 Almost eleven months to the day before the outbreak of World War II,

President Franklin Roosevelt stated the Four Freedoms he felt should prevail throughout the world. Can you name all four?

9 Walt Disney, the film giant, added his own Fifth Freedom to FDR's Four Freedoms. Can you name it?

10 At the first Olympic Winter Games, which were held in France, figure skater Sonja Henie, later to achieve motion picture fame, competed. Here's a three-part question on the skater-turned-actress. (a) What country did she represent, (b) how old was she, and (c) in what position did she finish?

11 One of the side effects of World War I was the establishment of Daylight Savings Time, which was continued following the war. What was the purpose for creating the "spring forward, fall back" policy?

12 The top-selling record of all time was written by Israel Baline, a Russian whose family emigrated to the United States when he was about five years old. By what name do we know him?

13 What was the reason for changing the name of the ancient city of Constantinople to Istanbul?

14 Little did Maria von Trapp know when she and her family fled from

Nazi-oppressed Austria in 1938 that their travails would become a smash Broadway musical and an ever-popular film. What movie details that escape?

15 The body of Poland's first prime minister, who took office in 1919, was not interred in his beloved homeland. He did not wish to be buried there until Poland was free. Who was Poland's first prime minister? (Hint: He was world famous for his nonpolitical profession.)

16 What independent entity was established by the Lateran Treaty of 1929?

17 Can you name the first president to set foot in Europe while in office?

18 The Russian Revolution of 1917 resulted in the overthrow and murder of Czar Nicholas II and his family, and the eventual takeover of Russia by the Soviets. In what year did the United States recognize the Soviet Union?

19 A book that was to make history was published in 1925 after a change of title. The author originally had planned to call it *Four and a Half Years of Struggle Against Lies, Stupidity and Cowardice*, but friends suggested a much shorter title. What was the book's final title?

20 On August 4, 1940, this founder of the Soviet Union was assassinated in Mexico City. Name him.

21 The Sinn Fein Party, whose leaders included Eamon de Valera, fought for many years to win independence for their nation. What nation is this?

22 We've all dreamed of finding that magical spot known as Shangri-la. Where is Shangri-la?

23 One of the leaders in the drive to gain independence for India from British control was Mohandas K. Gandhi (1869–1948). For twenty-one years prior to his return to India Gandhi lived in South Africa. What was his profession while in South Africa?

24 On December 10, 1936, Britain's King Edward VIII surrendered his crown to marry the woman he loved. What title did he then assume, and what was the name of the woman he married?

25 We hear much about the Big Four in the World War II era, but sometimes forget there was a Big Four at the Paris Peace Conference of 1919. Can you name the Big Four in that earlier parley and the quartet of nations they represented?

26 Germany was ruled by the Weimar Republic government with a democratic republican constitution until its president named Adolf Hitler as chancellor in 1933. Who was the German president who appointed Hitler?

27 Only one member of the Allied nations who defeated the Central Powers in World War I refused to sign the Versailles Treaty. Can you name the country?

28 The man who led the U.S. Senate drive to block the United States from joining the League of Nations was the grandfather of his namesake who served as an ambassador to the United Nations. Name them.

29 Let's try a variation on a "Who Said It?" question. "The Answer Man" will tell you who said it, but you must tell us the conditions under which it was said. King George V of Great Britain said: "How is the Empire?" Under what conditions did the king ask this question?

30 Regarding Hitler's book *Mein Kampf*: Where was it written?

31 Here's a "Name Her" question. Born in Virginia, her second husband was a British viscount. When he was elevated to the House of Lords, she became the first woman elected to the House of Commons. She was elected by a sizable majority on November 28, 1919. Name her.

32 In 1927 Charles A. Lindbergh made the first solo transatlantic flight. But, can you name the pair who made the first non-stop transatlantic flight in 1919?

33 Women were granted the right to vote nationally in 1920 in the United States. But what country was the first in the world to grant women's suffrage?

34 Speaking of "firsts," what country was the first to legalize abortion?

35 The Golden Age of Radio began in the twenties. The first public broadcast station was instituted in February 1920. Name the man who set it up, and the country in which it was established.

36 One of Adolf Hitler's first acts as president of the Nazi party was to establish the Gymnastic and Sports Division, which became the *Sturmabteilung*. By what name was this to become infamous?

37 Czech playwright Karel Capek gave the world a new word of importance both to science and especially science fiction in his 1921 play *R.U.R.* What was the word?

38 Here's a "Name Him" question. This son of a shoemaker might have become an Orthodox priest had he not been expelled from the seminary for his poor attitude. His original family name was Dzhugashvili, but he changed it to another that translates as "man of steel." (No, it's not Clark Kent by any means.) Name him.

39 Amelia Earhart (1898– 1937) was truly a pioneer in international aviation. Can you name the three most prominent "firsts" she accomplished in aviation history?

40 While we're on the subject of aviation innovations, can you name the first dirigible to complete a transatlantic commercial flight, and tell how long it took to accomplish its mission?

41 The German Workers' party, which was devised at the infamous 1923 gathering known as the "Beer Hall Putsch," is often referred to in stories of Adolf Hitler's rise to power. Who founded the German Workers' Party?

42 On October 30, 1938, a radio broadcast by Orson Welles stirred the fears of many who thought it was an actual news report. What was the name of that show?

43 The first scheduled transatlantic commercial air service took place in 1939. Can you name the airline and the points connected by the historic flight?

44 The Italians and Germans used the Spanish Civil War (1936–39) as a testing ground for armament and techniques they would later use in World War II. On what side would Spain later fight in World War II?

45 Almost two centuries after the American colonists' protest of Britain's tax on tea that led to the American Revolutionary War, Mohandas Gandhi led a famed march against another British tax in 1930. What product's taxation was the Indian leader protesting?

46 Speaking of marching, in 1934–35 China's Red Army staged what has become known as the Long March. Fleeing from the Nationalist Army some ninety thousand Communist men and women fled some six thousand miles, losing more than half their number. Who led the Long March?

Answers

1 *The League dissolved itself in 1946* after *the United Nations was established.*

2 *The well-intended Kellogg-Briand Pact outlawed war.*

3 *The* tang *in the word* Kuomintang *means party.*

④ *Jesse Owens (1913–1981) was the champion who took the medals, tying and breaking some Olympic records in the bargain.*

⑤ *Author of* Animal Farm *and* 1984 *to name but two of his works, Blair's nom de plume was George Orwell.*

⑥ *In 1930 Ras Tafari proclaimed himself emperor of Ethiopia and adopted the new name, Haile Selassie.*

⑦ *The first Winter Olympics were held in 1924.*

⑧ *They are Freedom of Speech, Religion, from Want, and from Fear.*

⑨ *Disney added Economic Freedom as a fifth freedom.*

⑩ *The (a) Norwegian, (b) eleven-year-old, finished (c) last in a field of eight.*

⑪ *It was intended as a means of conserving fuel by changing the time to make better use of daylight, thus cutting energy usage.*

⑫ *Israel Baline (1888–1989), who adopted the name Irving Berlin after it appeared on his first published song due to a printer's error, wrote* White Christmas.

⑬ *The name change was caused by strained relations between Turkey and*

Greece. Turkish Nationalists resented the name Constantinople's Greek connotations.

⑭ The Sound of Music *is based on the Von Trapp family's escape from the Nazis.*

⑮ *Ignace Jan Paderewski (1860–1941) is best known as the immortal pianist/composer of classical music. His casket was placed, "temporarily," in the base of the memorial to the USS* Maine *in Arlington National Cemetery in 1941. By the time you read this he may have been returned to his homeland.*

⑯ *The Lateran Treaty, signed by Benito Mussolini, established the Vatican as a city-state, ruled by the pope.*

⑰ *In 1918 Woodrow Wilson made history by traveling to Europe during his term as president.*

⑱ *The government of the Soviet Union was recognized by the United States in 1933, during Franklin Roosevelt's first administration.*

⑲ *The title, which when translated from German is* My Struggle, *will be more familiar to you as* Mein Kampf *by Adolf Hitler.*

⑳ *The former Communist leader, who had been exiled from the Soviet Union by* his Marxist peers in 1929, was Leon Trotsky (1879–1940). He was murdered with a mountain-climbing implement.

㉑ The Sinn Fein Party was important in the movement to gain Ireland's independence. Eamon de Valera, by the way, was born in the United States.

㉒ It's in the pages of a book. In other words, there's no such place as Shangri-la in the idyllic sense. It was created by James Hilton in his 1933 classic Lost Horizon.

㉓ While in South Africa, Gandhi practiced law.

㉔ King Edward VIII became the duke of Windsor and married the American divorcee Wallis Warfield Simpson.

㉕ The Big Four were France, represented by Prime Minister George Clemenceau, Great Britain's Prime Minister David Lloyd George, Italy's Prime Minister Vittorio Orlando, and U.S. President Woodrow Wilson.

㉖ Hitler, who suspended the constitution the very year he received his appointment, was put in office by Paul von Hindenburg (1847–1934). Ironically, von Hindenburg had defeated Hitler in the 1932 presidential election.

㉗ When German "rights" to Shantung Province were transferred to Japan, China walked out of the conference.

㉘ The grandfather/grandson were Senator Henry Cabot Lodge (1850–1924) and Henry Cabot Lodge, Jr. (1902–85). The younger Lodge also served as a senator from Massachusetts.

㉙ These were King George V's last words before he died on January 21, 1936.

㉚ Arrested for an attempted coup against the Bavarian government, Hitler wrote Mein Kampf during his nine-month prison stay.

㉛ It was Lady Nancy Witcher Astor (1879–1964).

㉜ The Vickers Vimy bomber was piloted across the Atlantic Ocean in 1919 by Royal Air Force Captain John Alcock. His navigator was Lieutenant Arthur Brown of the Royal Flying Corps.

㉝ The first nation to grant women's suffrage was New Zealand in 1893.

㉞ The Soviet Union legalized abortion in 1920.

㉟ It was Italian-born Guglielmo Marconi (1874–1937) who set up the first public broadcast station in Writtle, England.

㊱ *The* Sturmabteilung *will go down in infamy as the Stormtroopers.*

㊲ *It's the word* robot. R.U.R. *are the initials for* Rossum's Universal Robots.

㊳ *You know him as Josef Stalin (1879–1953), one of history's worst tyrants.*

㊴ *Earhart was the first woman passenger on a transatlantic flight (1928), the first female to fly solo on a transatlantic flight (1932), and the first pilot to fly solo from Hawaii to the U.S. mainland (1935).*

㊵ *In 1928, the* Graf Zeppelin *cruised from Germany to New Jersey in four and one-half days.*

㊶ *The German Workers' Party was founded by Anton Drexler. Hitler changed the party into the National Socialist German Workers' Party (Nazi Party).*

㊷ *Many will answer* The War of the Worlds, *but the H.G. Welles classic book that inspired the show was entitled* Invasion from Mars.

㊸ *Pan American Airways initiated service between Port Washington, Long Island, New York, and Lisbon, Portugal. Eleven years earlier Pan Am had also made the first commercial* *flight over international waters with a flight to the Caribbean.*

⑭ Spain, under the control of dictator Francisco Franco (1892–1975) was a nonbelligerent in World War II.

⑮ Gandhi led the 165 mile long Salt March of 1930, which was a protest against the tax on salt.

⑯ The Long March was led by the founder of the People's Republic of China Mao Tse-tung (1893–1976).

Back to the Battlefields

L*ess than two dec-
ades after the end of World War I, the
world again found itself facing a would-
be world conqueror, Adolf Hitler. Along
with Italy and Japan, Germany once
more was sending its military forces into
neighboring lands with an eye on conquest. Before long virtually all the great
world powers and many of the lesser
states were locked in a worldwide conflict that began in 1939 and ended in
1945, with a death toll higher than that
of any other war in history.*

❶ In September 1939,
after a long, valiant resistance, Warsaw, Poland, fell
to Hitler's Nazi hordes. As a final act of defiance,
what composer's music was continuously broadcast

over Warsaw radio? Real history and/or music buffs can take a shot at naming the particular work that was being broadcast.

❷ Can you name the World War II liquid-fuel German rocket bomb that is considered the forerunner to today's ballistic missile?

❸ During World War II the Japanese government, in desperation, formed a Special Attack Force whose mission was to destroy U.S. aircraft carriers. The method was suicidal dives onto the decks of the ships. Members of the force were called the "Kamikaze." What does kamikaze mean?

❹ In World War II what was referred to by the Japanese as their "unsinkable aircraft carrier"?

❺ Who fired the first shot when the Japanese launched their attack on Pearl Harbor, bringing the United States into World War II—Japan or the United States?

❻ Hitler was known for the misery he wrought on the world, and on the Germany he ruled with an iron hand. But Hitler was not German by birth. Where was he born?

7 Adolf Hitler is sometimes referred to—erroneously—by another surname. What is it?

8 Is the international radiotelephone distress signal *Mayday* in any way connected with May 1, which was celebrated as a festive day in past centuries and currently by Socialist and Communist groups?

9 In World War II the Japanese turned in desperation to the use of Ohka bombs. What was unique about Ohka bombs?

10 Among history's most tragic events are the Nazi atrocities against the Jews in Auschwitz during World War II. In what country was the Auschwitz Concentration Camp?

11 On December 7, 1941, when the Japanese staged the infamous sneak attack on U.S. forces in Pearl Harbor, what was Hawaii's status vis-à-vis the United States?

12 The famed cartoon strip "The Captain and the Kids" originally had a different name, but World War II caused it to be changed. What was the strip's original name?

13 On April 9, 1942, U.S. forces in the Philippines, under Major General Edward King, Jr., were forced to surrender to the Japanese Imperial Army. Can you name the famed peninsula on which this surrender took place?

14 Name the multinational body, established to help nations through short-term financial problems, that resulted from the 1944 Bretton Woods conference.

15 Another entity that traces its existence to the Bretton Woods conference is the International Bank for Reconstruction and Development. However, it has a more commonly used name. What is the other name for the International Bank for Reconstruction and Development?

16 In a battle off Formosa (October 13–16, 1944), U.S. Admiral William Halsey lured the Japanese into a trap that destroyed more than 650 of their planes. By what name do we know the island of Formosa?

17 This German, considered one of the most brilliant generals in World War II, allegedly was forced to take poison because of his part in a plot to kill Adolf Hitler. Name him.

18 Which was nicknamed the "Great War": World War I or World War II?

19 Japanese soldiers often cried out the word *Banzai* when launching assaults on Allied troops. What does the word mean?

20 The getaway spot used by President Franklin Roosevelt during World War II is now known as Camp David in Maryland. Do you know what FDR originally named it?

21 Relative to the preceding question, who changed the name of the mountain retreat to Camp David?

22 Italian dictator Benito Mussolini came to an ignominious end. He and his mistress were taken by a mob, shot, and hung by the heels. In what city did this occur?

23 On November 9, 1938, *Kristallnacht*, the Nazis launched a full-scale assault on German Jews, imprisoning some 20,000 and killing one hundred. What does *Kristallnacht* mean, and why was this term applied to the brutal assault?

24 Name the man who was proclaimed emperor of Vietnam by the Japanese toward the end of World War II.

25 A major engineering accomplishment was the construction by Chinese laborers of an 800-mile land route between India and China in 1937–38. The roadway was of great importance in the transporting of supplies during World War II. By what name do we know this highway?

26 He came to be known by his umbrella and derby cap and the phrase "peace for our time." Who was he?

27 Here's a "Name Him" question. In 1940 the French Vichy government, which had capitulated to Nazi Germany, broke relations with Britain. The World War I hero, who nominally headed the Vichy government, was convicted of treason and sentenced to death following World War II. His sentence was later commuted to life, and he died in prison. Name him.

28 Of the two leading Axis powers of World War II, which surrendered first, Germany or Japan?

29 The morale of Allied service personnel in World War II was boosted greatly by USO tours, including such entertainers as Bob Hope and introducing the USO's famed "Stagedoor Canteens." What do the initials USO represent?

30 In July 1941 President Franklin Roosevelt, concerned about the threatening international security problems, appointed William "Wild Bill" Donovan to head up a new civilian agency, the Office of Strategic Services (OSS). By what name do we now know this organization?

31 During World War II the BBC (British Broadcasting Corporation) began broadcasts into Europe urging the formation of resistance forces. They adopted a slogan which has become international, using a Morse Code signal. What was that signal? (Hint: It lent itself well to a hand signal.)

32 Among the many reprehensible Nazi acts against Jews was the requirement that all Jews over the age of six be marked for identification. What mark was forced on the Jews?

33 His series of radio messages inspired his nation. In the first of these he uttered the phrase, "I have nothing to offer you but blood, toil, tears, and sweat." Who was this internationally famous world leader: (a) Clement Atlee, (b) Winston Churchill, (c) Charles de Gaulle, or (d) Franklin Roosevelt?

34 Four years before the United States entered World War II, an American pilot journeyed to China to help Chiang Kai-shek organize the Chinese air force against the invading Japanese. Who was this man who founded the famed Flying Tigers?

35 Of the three main Axis nations, only the emperor of Japan survived the conclusion of World War II. Who was Japan's emperor?

36 One of the major failures of Nazi Germany in World War II was Operation Barbarossa. What was Operation Barbarossa?

37 Their failure to act in the face of warnings of an attack on Pearl Harbor resulted in the dismissal of two military leaders in charge of the U.S. forces in Hawaii. Name the two commanders.

38 You've earned an easy question. What date was marked by President Franklin Roosevelt as "a day that will live in infamy"?

39 Was the vote unanimous in the U.S. Congress to declare war on Japan?

40 Relative to the preceding question, did Congress declare war on Germany, Italy, and Japan all at the same time?

41 In 1939 Adolf Hitler and Joseph Stalin formed a Russo-German non-agression pact that was violated when Hitler's forces invaded the Soviet Union on June 22, 1941. What battle is considered the turning point in driving back the Nazi assault?

42 Sword, Gold, Juno, Omaha, and Utah—to what do these words refer in an historic context?

43 Fear of Axis terrorism in the United States due to the troubled world situation resulted in the creation of the U.S. Office of Civilian Defense. Who was named to be assistant director of the Office of Civilian Defense in 1941?

44 One of the most horrendous aspects of World War II was the "Final Solution," in which Hitler ordered that all Jews be taken to extermination camps. Who was the SS officer charged with carrying out this atrocity?

45 Where did the term *quisling*, meaning traitor, originate?

46 What was the Nazi's Operation Sea Lion in World War II?

47 Howell M. Forgy, the chaplain on the U.S. cruiser *New Orleans*, spurred on his shipmates during the attack on Pearl Harbor with a phrase that was often repeated during the war. In fact, it was later set to music. Can you guess the phrase?

48 General Douglas MacArthur was renowned for coining timeless phrases. What territory was he leaving when he voiced the famous remark, "I shall return"?

49 In 1942 RCA Victor presented the first gold record to an artist for sales topping the million mark. The performer added to his fame with his service in World War II. Can you name the record and the performer?

50 The Battle of Britain, launched by Adolf Hitler in 1940, saw raids of up to 1,000 planes daily against Great Britain. This was a prime example of the Germans' blitzkrieg. What does *blitzkrieg* mean?

51 Casualties from the German air assaults during the Battle of Britain were lessened somewhat by the first use of radar to warn of aerial approaches. Where did radar get its name?

52 Here's a "Name Him" question. He was born on November 22, 1890. On the day following the announcement by his homeland's leader that the nation had surrendered to Adolf Hitler, he went on the air in London with an appeal to his countrymen not to surrender. With daily broadcasts, he won recognition from the British as the head of his country's government in exile. In 1945 the citizens cheered as he paraded through the liberated capital of his native land. Name him.

53 The Maginot Line was supposed to be impregnable to any Nazi attack, but proved ineffective. Between what two countries did the Maginot Line extend?

54 Even the evil have love affairs. What famous despot called Eva Braun his loved one?

55 What was the first foreign nation to fall to Nazi Germany? It was conquered in March 1938.

56 An important element in the Germans' conduct of the Battle of the Atlantic was the submarine known as the U-boat. What does the name U-boat mean?

57 In 1949 Iva Toguri D'Aquino was found guilty and sentenced to ten years in prison for her activities during World War II. She served six years before her release on good behavior. On what charge was D'Aquino tried?

58 It was during World War II that the largest volunteer army in history was assembled. What country's citizenry comprised this vast group of volunteers?

59 One of Hitler's closest aides was the man he appointed as propaganda minister in 1933. When the Nazis fell to the Allies, this master of the "Big Lie" killed his family and committed suicide. Name him.

60 In December 1944 the Germans staged a last-ditch attack against U.S. forces in the Belgian-Luxembourg sector, actually placing a dent in the Allied lines before the gap was closed and the German armies were checked. By what name does history mark this final assault in the West?

61 The man who approved the attack on Pearl Harbor later attempted suicide and failed. Following the war, he was convicted as a war criminal and hanged. Who was this Japanese premier?

62 D-Day, June 6, 1944, was the largest seaborne invasion in history, marking the launching of the final Allied campaign of the European phase of World War II. For what operation was D-Day the code name?

63 When the Germans prepared their forces for the invasion of the Soviet Union in June 1941, what type of clothing was *not* included?

64 What was the secret code broadcast to Japanese aircraft carriers ordering the sneak attack on Pearl Harbor?

65 *Little Boy* and *Fat Man* were decisive in drawing the Pacific phase of World War II to an end. Who or what were Little Boy and Fat Man?

66 Who led the British forces that finally drove Field Marshal Erwin Rommel's Afrika Korps out of Egypt in 1943, a campaign highlighted by the Germans' defeat at El Alamein?

67 Despite heavy bombardment by German forces, 345,000 British and French troops were evacuated from a French port between May 29 and June 4, 1940. The evacuation was called *Operation Dynamo*. What was the name of that historic port?

68 What role did Indian leader Mohandas Gandhi play in World War II?

Answers

① *It was that of Frederic Chopin, who a century before had fled his homeland to escape the czar's domination. Chopin's* Polonaise in A Major *was the last defiant work broadcast as the Nazis took control.*

② *It was the V-2. The "V" stood for vengeance. Hitler sent the first "flying bombs," the V-1, over London on June 13, 1944, soon after D-Day.*

③ *Kamikaze means "divine wind." The term originated in the thirteenth century when a typhoon—a Divine Wind—virtually destroyed Mongol ships attempting an invasion of Japan.*

④ *The unsinkable aircraft carrier was the island of Formosa, which was then a Japanese colony in the Formosa Straits.*

⑤ *The crew of the destroyer U.S.S.* Ward *dropped a depth charge on a Japanese submarine in Hawaiian waters an hour before Japanese aircraft attacked Pearl Harbor on December 7, 1941.*

⑥ *Hitler was born in Braunau am Inn, Austria-Hungary.*

⑦ *Hitler's father was illegitimate and for a time he used his mother's maiden name, Schicklgruber, as his surname. The father had laid claim to the name Hitler prior to Adolf's birth.*

⑧ *No; it's a takeoff on the French word* m'aidez, *which translates as "help me."*

⑨ *The Ohka bombs were rocket-like weapons to which human beings were attached—the dreaded kamikaze, suicide pilots, who guided their bombs into their targets.*

⑩ *Auschwitz is in Poland.*

⑪ *Hawaii was a territory of the United States in 1941.*

⑫ *"The Katzenjammer Kids" was name-changed because of the Nazis and World War II. There was fear of public reaction to the German name.*

⑬ *It was on Bataan, and led to the infamous Bataan Death March, which took the lives of 5,200-plus U.S. soldiers and even more Filipinos.*

⑭ *The multi-national financial institution is the International Monetary Fund (IMF).*

⑮ *You probably know it by its shorter name, the World Bank.*

⑯ *Formosa, which means "beautiful," was the Portuguese name for what we now know as Taiwan, which is controlled by the Republic of China.*

⑰ *It was the "Desert Fox," Field Marshal Erwin Rommel, who led the Afrika Korps.*

⑱ *World War I has the dubious honor of being labeled the "Great War."*

⑲ *It means "10,000 years," the Japanese equivalent of "Viva" or "Long Live the King."*

⑳ *He called it Shangri-la.*

㉑ *President Dwight Eisenhower changed Shangri-la's name to Camp David, in honor of his grandson.*

㉒ *Mussolini, or* Il Duce, *as he liked to be called, met his just rewards in Milan.*

㉓ Kristallnacht *means "night of crystal," or night of broken glass. It was so named because the windows in synagogues and Jewish homes and businesses were broken by rock-throwing Nazis.*

㉔ *The last emperor of Vietnam was Bao Dai (1926–45).*

㉕ *It was the Burma Road, which was blocked by the Japanese in May 1942.*

㉖ *British Prime Minister Neville Chamberlain (1869–1940), whose efforts to save the peace ended in utter failure.*

㉗ *The Vichy government was headed by Marshal Henri Pétain (1856–1951).*

㉘ *Germany surrendered on May 8, 1945. The Japanese held out until September 2 of that year.*

㉙ *The USO, founded in February 1941, is the United Service Organization.*

㉚ *The OSS was the forerunner to the Central Intelligence Agency, or CIA.*

㉛ *The BBC transmitted the Morse Code for the letter* V, *which evolved into the slogan "V for Victory." This resulted in the paint-*

ing of the letter "V" on walls and the two-finger "V" hand signal. In addition, the opening notes of Beethoven's Fifth Symphony were often played because they correspond to the "dot, dot, dot, dash," which is the Morse Code for the letter "V."

㉜ *All Jews in Nazi-occupied countries were to have a yellow Star of David sewn onto their clothing.*

㉝ *(b) It was British Prime Minister Winston Churchill.*

㉞ *The American aviator was Claire Chennault (1890–1958).*

㉟ *Hirohito was emperor of Japan. In 1946 he renounced imperial divinity and adopted a ceremonial leadership role.*

㊱ *Operation Barbarossa was the German attack on the Soviet Union, which severed the Nazi-Soviet Non-Aggression Pact.*

㊲ *They were Admiral Husband E. Kimmel, commander in chief of the Pacific Fleet, and General Walter C. Short, U.S. Army commander in Hawaii. Some historians believe the two were scapegoats for their superiors who were responsible for ignoring the warnings.*

㊳ *The day, which resulted in the battle cry, "Remember Pearl Harbor," was December 7, 1941.*

③⑨ *No. The Senate vote was 82–0, but the vote in the House of Representatives was 388–1. The lone House member who voted against the war was Representative Jeannette Rankin, R-Mont. Rankin, the first woman ever elected to the House, had also voted against declaring war in World War I in 1917.*

④⓪ *No. Congress declared war on Japan on December 8, 1941. Germany and Italy declared war on the United States on December 11, and Congress returned the favor that same day.*

④① *It was the Battle of Stalingrad, which ended in February 1943 with an estimated casualty rate of 330,000 for the Germans.*

④② *These were the code names for the five allied beachheads in the World War II D-Day invasion of Nazi-occupied France.*

④③ *You would know her better if we asked, "Who was the first lady in 1941?" The answer is Eleanor Roosevelt.*

④④ *The exterminations were directed by Gestapo Lieutenant Colonel Adolf Eichmann, who escaped to Argentina following the war. He was finally abducted, taken to Israel, tried, and executed in 1962.*

④⑤ *Vidkun Quisling (1887–1945) was a fascist who aided the German invasion* of his native Norway. His reward from Hitler was appointment as premier of a puppet government. He was later rewarded by being executed for treason.

46 *Operation Sea Lion was an unsuccessful Nazi plan for the invasion of Great Britain.*

47 *While the sailors were engaged in maintaining their antiaircraft operations, Forgy repeated the words "Praise the Lord, and pass the ammunition."*

48 *It was on March 11, 1942, when he was leaving the Philippines.*

49 *The gold record went to the immortal band leader Major Glenn Miller (1904–44), who died while serving in the Army Air Corps. The song was "Chattanooga Choo Choo."*

50 Blitzkrieg, *an intensive aerial bombing, means lightning war.*

51 *Radar is an acronym for* radio detection and ranging.

52 *It was Charles de Gaulle of France, who will soon be honored with a statue facing Paris's Arc de Triomphe.*

53 *The Maginot Line was situated on the frontier between France and Germany.*

54 *Eva Braun was Adolf Hitler's mistress. The mass murderer and the woman whom he had just married committed suicide together as World War II ground to an end.*

55 *Austria, Adolf Hitler's birthplace, was the first Nazi conquest.*

56 *It's actually quite easy. The U-boat was called an* Unterseeboot, *or undersea boat. Hence the name U-boat.*

57 *D'Aquino was convicted of treason. She was one of thirteen women who aired propaganda messages to U.S. service personnel in the Pacific Theater under the pseudonym Tokyo Rose. In 1977 President Gerald Ford granted her a pardon on the grounds that she had been wrongly accused.*

58 *It was India.*

59 *John Joseph Goebbels (1897–1945) was the Hitlerite who controlled the German media, including theater and cinema.*

60 *Named for the dent in the Allied lines, this is known as the Battle of the Bulge.*

61 *The convicted war criminal was General Hideki Tojo (1884–1948).*

⑥② *The landing of Allied forces, 120,000 strong, on five beaches on the coast of Normandy, France, was termed* Operation Overlord.

⑥③ *The cocky Nazi military leaders did not include winter garb. They didn't think the campaign would take that long.*

⑥④ *The carriers were ordered to "Climb Mount Nikata."*

⑥⑤ *They were nuclear bombs. Little Boy was the uranium bomb dropped on Hiroshima by the* Enola Gay *on August 6, 1945. Little Boy was the plutonium bomb dropped on Nagasaki three days later.*

⑥⑥ *The British were commanded by Bernard Law Montgomery, or First Viscount Montgomery of Alamein (1887–1976).*

⑥⑦ *Operation Dynamo took place at Dunkirk in northern France. With the Germans closing in and the Allied troops' only escape being to cross the English Channel, the British organized what became an armada of transports and civilian craft, and every available boat was pressed into service.*

⑥⑧ *In keeping with his pacifism, the Indian leader refused to lend his cooperation to the war effort and in 1942 the British jailed him. He was released in 1944 as a result of public support for him.*

The Postwar
Turns Chilly

In the wake of World War II the world faced a period of great change. Europe was divided into two armed camps—East and West. Asia also underwent massive changes, but in the Orient the divisions were more North and South—North and South Korea, North and South Vietnam.

The vast European empires began to collapse and one by one countries in Africa, Asia, and the Middle East gained their independence.

There were also enormous technological advances—vastly improved communications, television, space exploration, and jet travel—advances that continue into the next chapter and to the present day.

1 Name the conference at which the leaders of the World War II superpowers—Great Britain, the Soviet Union, and the United States—agreed on the postwar occupation of Germany.

2 In what year did Israel become an independent nation?

3 Throughout history many countries have undergone name changes. Here's a "Match 'em" question for you. Match these countries with their former names:

Current Name	Former Name
1. Iran	(a) Belgian Congo
2. Iraq	(b) Helvetia
3. Switzerland	(c) Mesopotamia
4. Zaire	(d) Persia
5. Zimbabwe	(e) Rhodesia

4 On January 1, 1959, this island-nation fell to a revolutionary who later declared himself to be a Communist. Name the troubled country.

5 Here's a "Name Him" question. This great grandson of an Italian immigrant twice ruled a Latin American nation. Elected to a first term, he created a dictatorship, was unseated in a military coup, then returned to power two decades later. Name him.

6 When the dictator in the preceding question died in office, who succeeded him as president?

7 The Nuremberg Trials marked the first time in history that those who had led the world into war were placed on trial for their acts. There were three classes of what were designated as "war crimes." Can you name them?

8 How many defendants were tried at the Nuremberg Trials, and how many of them were condemned to death?

9 In the post-World War II era, there was much ado about the "Big Three" nations. Which nations were the Big Three?

10 The Association of Southeast Asian Nations (ASEAN) was formed in 1967. Can you name the six current ASEAN members?

11 In 1975 thirty-five nations signed the Helsinki Final Act (or Helsinki Accords), which supposedly was to further the cause of human rights in those nations. The signers included the United States, Canada, the Soviet Union, and all the nations of East and West Europe, except one. Can you guess which European nation is the lone non-signer?

⑫ In 1969 the first Nobel Prize in a new category was presented, the first category added since the original five. What was that new award category?

⑬ How many nations (not counting North and South Korea) were engaged in combat in the Korean War?

⑭ Here's a "Name Him" question. Since taking power in Cuba, Fidel Castro has been spreading leftist revolution in Latin America. One of his earliest accomplices was killed attempting to organize a revolution in Bolivia in 1967. Name him. (For extra credit, this Castroite was not born in Cuba. Where was he born?)

⑮ The two most powerful men in the People's Republic of China, both veterans of the Long March, died in 1976. Can you name these founders of the Chinese Communist party?

⑯ On June 3, 1946, the Reard Company of Paris, founded by Louis Reard, introduced a fashion innovation that shook the world, both fashion wise and socially. What was this new style?

⑰ In 1964 this Soviet, who held office as both premier and party secretary, was replaced. Who was this Kremlin chief, and, for extra credit, who were the two men who displaced him?

18 Among the petty, but ruthless, rulers who sprang up in the post-World War II era was Idi Amin, who in 1976 was named president for life of a central African country. That "life presidency," however, was thankfully short. In 1979 Amin had to flee the country. Can you name this country?

19 Throughout the decades of Soviet rule over Russia, we often heard reports of forced-labor prison camps. What are these Russian prison camps called?

20 The Soviets reportedly timed the October 4, 1957, launching of Sputnik I to coincide with the 100th anniversary of the birth of Konstantin E. Tsiolkovsky (1857–1935). Who was Tsiolkovsky, and for what should he be remembered?

21 Name the secretary-general of the United Nations who was killed in a plane crash in 1961 in the Congo.

22 In 1989 many visitors to Berlin collected chips from the crumbling symbol of communism's failure to win over the people—the Berlin Wall. In what year was the infamous Wall erected?

㉓ The phrase "Iron Curtain" was initiated in a speech made on March 5, 1946, at Westminster College in Fulton, Missouri. Who gave that speech and, thus, created the descriptive phrase?

㉔ Name the two men who made history in 1953 by being the first to reach the summit of Mount Everest, the world's highest mountain.

㉕ "The Answer Man" will name three Communist officials. You are to tell which country each ruled: (a) Klement Gottwald, (b) Imre Nagy, and (c) Josip Broz, known as Marshal Tito.

㉖ "The Answer Man" is going to give you two famous London street addresses. Your job is to tell us who lives at each address: (a) 221B Baker Street, and (b) 10 Downing Street.

㉗ We often hear mention of Interpol, especially in fiction stories. What is Interpol?

㉘ The founding of the United Nations was a result of agreements made at an international meeting held February 4–11, 1945. Can you identify that meeting?

㉙ Although this early Communist party leader and foreign minister was later discredited, even to the point of having his name removed from places of honor (buildings and towns named after him), his name is still mentioned quite often albeit mostly in stressful situations. Who is this Bolshevik?

30 Who was the leader of the Vietnamese Communists in both the French-Indochina War (1946–54) and the Vietnam War (from 1961 until his death in 1969)?

31 There were five official working U.N. languages adopted when the organization was created. Can you name them?

32 One official language was added by the U.N. General Assembly in 1973 and by the Security Council in 1982. What language was this?

33 There is an estate in the nation's capital known as Dumbarton Oaks. Of what significance is this mansion to world political history?

34 The International Court of Justice, which was established in 1946 to administer justice under international law, sits at The Hague in the Netherlands. How many judges serve on this court?

35 The cutback in colonialism in southern Africa has seen the rise of many black nations. In 1964 Kenya, Tanzania, and Zambia all had new black presidents. Can you name the first president of each of these newly formed nations, respectively?

36 By what name do we know the European Recovery Plan?

37 Khmer Rouge may sound to some like an item of facial makeup. Far from it. What is (are) the *Khmer Rouge*?

38 In what city was the first session of the U.N. General Assembly held?

39 In 1952 an operation was performed in Denmark on George Jorgenson, an American, that made history and roused quite a few headlines ... and eyebrows. What was this operation?

40 Nguyen That Thanh may not be a familiar name to you, but his place in the history of Southeast Asia is assured. What name did Nguyen That Thanh adopt and make infamous?

41 In order to prove his theory that Polynesia could have been settled originally by South American natives, this Norwegian sailed in a raft from Peru to the South Pacific island in 1947. Can you name the daring adventurer and his balsa wood raft? (Hint: A book, describing the adventure, bore the craft's name as its title.)

42 This answer may surprise you. The first tape recorder for home use and the first microwave oven made their debut in the same year. What year was it?

43 Here's a "Mini-Match 'em" question. Syngman Rhee and Kim Il Sung were leaders of the respective Korean republics—North (Korean People's Democratic Republic) and South (Republic of Korea). Which was president of North Korea (Communist), and which was president of South Korea?

44 When he was twenty, David Green left his homeland, Poland, and in 1949 became prime minister of his adopted nation. By what name does history know David Green?

45 In what country did the rebellious Huks wreak havoc for many years, even to the point of killing the widow of the nation's president?

46 Arguably the biggest news story during the Korean War was President Harry Truman's removal of the general who headed the forces there. For this two-parter, name (a) the general who was replaced and (b) the general who replaced him.

47 One of the most publicized spy cases ever was uncovered in Great Britain in the early fifties when three foreign service officials fled to the Soviet Union to avoid arrest as espionage agents. Can you name these traitors?

48 What nations were involved in what has become known as the "Six Day War"?

49 Who became the first prime minister of India when it became independent?

50 Who ruled Libya at the time of the September 1969 coup that resulted in the rise to power of Colonel Moammar Gadhafi?

51 Who was the first president of the Republic of (South) Vietnam?

52 On April 12, 1961, a barrier was broken when the first manned spacecraft orbited the earth. Who was the cosmonaut, and what was the name of the spacecraft?

53 In what country did the word "brainwashing" originate to describe mental stress used as a means to force a change in beliefs?

54 Here's a two-part question on Sri Lanka, which gained independence from Great Britain in 1948: (a) What was Sri Lanka's name when it was a British colony, and (b) do you know what the words Sri Lanka mean?

55 In 1960 Sirimavo Bandaronaike made history when she became the world's first woman prime minister. Of what nation was Bandaronaike prime minister (1960–65, 1970–77)?

56 In 1946 the "autonomous Republic of Cochin China" was established. Where is (was) Cochin China?

57 How many members were there in the United Nations at its beginning?

Answers

① *It was the Yalta Conference, held in the Crimea, February 4–11, 1945.*

② *Israel officially became a nation on May 14, 1948.*

③ *1(d) Iran/Persia, 2(c) Iraq/Mesopotamia, 3(b) Switzerland/Helvetia, 4(a) Zaire/Belgian Congo, and 5(e) Zimbabwe/Rhodesia.*

④ *It was on January 1, 1959, that Fulgencio Batista resigned as president of Cuba and fled, turning over the rule of the island-nation to Fidel Castro.*

⑤ *Juan Domingo Peron (1895–1974), president of Argentina (1946–55, 1973–74).*

⑥ *Peron was succeeded by his vice president, Maria Estela Martinez de Peron, his third wife.*

⑦ *The three classes are crimes against peace, such as planning or waging a war of aggression; crimes against humanity, such as extermination, enslavement, deportation, and other inhumane acts; and war crimes, which are violations of the accepted laws and customs of warfare.*

⑧ *After holding 403 public sessions and hearing hundreds of witnesses, twelve of the original twenty-four defendants were condemned to death by hanging.*

⑨ *Great Britain, the Union of Soviet Socialist Republics, and the United States were the Big Three. The representatives of each were British Prime Minister Winston Churchill, Soviet Premier Joseph Stalin, and U.S. President Harry S Truman.*

⑩ *The six current ASEAN members are Brunei Darussalam, Indonesia, Malaysia, the Philippines, Singapore, and Thailand. Papua New Guinea has observer status.*

⑪ *Albania has the distinction of being the only European nation not to sign the Helsinki Accords.*

⑫ *The Nobel Prize in Economic Science was added in 1969.*

⑬ *On the North Korean side: one. On the South Korean side: fifteen.*

⑭ *It was Castro's longtime associate Ernesto "Che" Guevara, who was born in Argentina.*

⑮ *The Communist leaders were Chou En-lai (1898–1976), who was premier of the PRC when he died on January 8, and Mao Tsetung (1893–1976), the most powerful man in Mainland China, who died on September 9.*

⑯ *It was the Bikini bathing suit, which was named for the "ultimate impact" of the A-bomb test on Bikini Atoll.*

⑰ *Nikita Khruschev was replaced as Communist party secretary by Leonid Brezhnev and as premier by Aleksei Kosygin.*

⑱ *Idi Amin was the would-be president for life of the Republic of Uganda.*

⑲ *They are called* gulags. Gulag *is actually an acronym for Chief Administration of Corrective Labor Camps, which is a department of the KGB (Soviet secret police).*

⑳ *Tsiolkovsky was a Russian math teacher who devised some of the funda-*

mental principles of space flight, including the use of liquid propellant in place of gunpowder to achieve greater thrust. He also built one of the first wind tunnels.

㉑ *The secretary-general was Dag Hammarskjold (1905–61).*

㉒ *It was erected in 1961.*

㉓ *Sir Winston Churchill addressed an audience at Westminster by invitation of President Harry Truman. Said Churchill, "From Stettin in the Baltic to Trieste in the Adriatic, an iron curtain has descended across the continent [of Europe]."*

㉔ *Sir Edmund Hillary of New Zealand and Tenzing Norkey of Nepal conquered the Himalayan peak.*

㉕ *(a) Gottwald ruled in Czechoslovakia, (b) Nagy in Hungary, and (c) Tito in Yugoslavia.*

㉖ *(a) Nobody lives at 221B Baker Street. This is the fictional address of Sir Arthur Conan Doyle's master detective, Sherlock Holmes. (b) This address, 10 Downing Street, is the official residence of Britain's prime ministers.*

㉗ *Interpol is the acronym for the International Criminal Police Commission. The international clearinghouse for police informa-*

tion, created in Vienna in 1923, was reconstituted and moved to Paris in 1946.

㉘ *It was the Yalta Conference. The concept for a U.N.-type organization was initiated with the Atlantic Charter of 1941.*

㉙ *Vyacheslav Molotov (1890–1983) is the man for whom the "Molotov cocktail" was named.*

㉚ *The communist leader was Ho Chi Minh (1890–1969).*

㉛ *The languages are Chinese, English, French, Russian, and Spanish.*

㉜ *Arabic.*

㉝ *It was at the Dumbarton Oaks Conference that representatives of the "Big Four"—China (pre-Communist), the Soviet Union, the United Kingdom, and the host-nation United States—met to take the first steps toward establishing a permanent U.N. organization.*

㉞ *It has fifteen judges.*

㉟ *Kenya's first president was Jomo Kenyatta, Tanzania's was Julius Nyerere, and Zambia's was Kenneth Kaunda. All took office in 1964.*

㊱ *The European Recovery Plan was nicknamed the Marshall Plan in honor of its chief proponent, Secretary of State George Marshall.*

(37) *The Khmer Rouge are the ruthless Communist guerillas of Cambodia or, as they call it, Kampuchea. When they gained control of Cambodia in 1977 they forced people to leave the cities and killed the educated, the middle class, the Buddhist priests, and anyone else of power, authority, or uniqueness in the society. From 1977 to 1985 it is estimated that some 4 million Cambodians died at the hands of the Khmer Rouge.*

(38) *The first U.N. General Assembly meeting was held on January 10, 1946, in London.*

(39) *That operation turned George Jorgenson into Christine Jorgenson. It was the first sex-change operation in history.*

(40) *You might know Nguyen That Thanh better as the Communist leader of the North Vietnamese, Ho Chi Minh (1890–1969).*

(41) *Thor Heyerdahl made the trip with five companions on the* Kon Tiki.

(42) *Both electronic instruments went on the market in 1947.*

(43) *Rhee was the first South Korean president, and Sung was the first president of North Korea.*

㊹ *David Green became the first prime minister of Israel, his adopted nation, after changing his name to David Ben-Gurion (1886–1973).*

㊺ *On April 28, 1949, the Huks (People's Liberation Army) murdered Aurora Quezon, widow of Manuel Quezon, the first president of the Philippines.*

㊻ *(a) General Douglas MacArthur was replaced by (b) General Matthew Ridgway.*

㊼ *The traitors were Guy Burgess, Donald Maclean, and Kim Philby, who all defected. A fourth person involved was Sir Anthony Blunt, who was stripped of his knighthood and retired.*

㊽ *In June 1967 Israeli planes attacked airfields in Egypt, Jordan, and Syria. Israel's six day victory gave the young nation control over the Sinai Peninsula, Jerusalem, the West Bank of the Jordan River, and the Golan Heights.*

㊾ *Jawaharlal Nehru (1889–1964) rose to lead India after it was freed of British control in 1947.*

㊿ *Gadhafi unseated King Idris I, who had ruled since 1951.*

(51) *The first president of the Republic of Vietnam was Ngo Dinh Diem (1901–63), who was assassinated in 1963.*

(52) *The Soviet astronaut was Yuri Alekseyevich Gagarin (1934–68). Gagarin spent one and a half hours orbiting the earth in* Vostok I.

(53) *According to the late Edward Hunter, author of* Brainwashing *and* Brainwashing in Red China, *it was first used in the People's Republic of China.*

(54) *(a) Ceylon changed its name to Sri Lanka (actually it merely reverted to its traditional name). (b) It means resplendent island.*

(55) *Sri Lanka.*

(56) *Cochin China is part of Vietnam. It was established in a futile bid to thwart the Vietnamese Communists.*

(57) *Although there was a loosely tied group in World War II that was called the United Nations, the body we know by that name was organized in 1945 with fifty-one members.*

And the Walls Came Tumblin' Down

Τhe world contin- *ues to turn—both on its axis and in the evolutionary sense. Recent years have seen amazing changes, the fall of the Iron Curtain being perhaps the most historically important.*

These interesting—and ongoing— changes will fuel future editions of Who, What, When, Where, Why in the World of World History. *Let's look now at some questions on our most recent period in history.*

❶ One of the first East European nations to overturn Communist rule was Poland. The drive for freedom in Poland was led by *Solidarnosc*. What is *Solidarnosc*?

❷ In 1979 Soviet Union troops invaded Afghanistan, launching a decade of brutal warfare in an attempt to overcome the Afghan freedom fighters. During that conflict, an oft-heard word was *Jihad*. What does this word mean?

❸ Despite its having been outlawed, thirty-two persons were arrested in 1990 in India for performing a ritual known as *suttee* (sometimes spelled *sati*). What is this forbidden rite?

❹ Although the United States doesn't officially recognize the Chinese government on the island-province of Taiwan, there are indeed two nations calling themselves "China." Their initials are ROC and PRC. Spelled out, what do these two sets of initials denote? Which is on Taiwan and which is Mainland China?

❺ Among the guerrilla movements of the 1980s was one formed in Nicaragua in an attempt to take control of that Latin American nation from the rule of the Sandinistas. The guerrillas were called the *contras*. What does the word *contra* mean?

❻ Related to the preceding question, where did the name *Sandinistas* originate?

7 A growing fad in the United States in the 1990s, inherited from Asia, is the *karaoke*. What is a karaoke?

8 Margaret Roberts is an important personality in British history. Who is Margaret Roberts, you ask? That's precisely the question.

9 The Republic of Vanuatu became independent in 1980. What is the former name of this republic?

10 President Vigdis Finnbogadottir of Iceland enjoys an historic international distinction. What is it?

11 In the wake of the collapse of the Iron Curtain in 1990, a classic U.S. motion picture made its debut in the Soviet Union under the title, *Unesennye Vetrom*. What is the English-language title of the film?

12 Among the many (and still ongoing) changes in the Soviet Union was the election in 1990 of a president of the Russian Republic. Shortly after this election he resigned from the Communist party. Who is this Russian renegade?

13 The world's oldest republic, dating since 1569, consists of about 23.6 square miles of land space. Can you name it?

14 When Mikhail Gorbachev succeeded Konstantin Chernenko as leader of the Soviet Union he liberalized control over the Eastern Bloc. The words that leaped into the headlines around the world were *glasnost* and *perestroika*. What do these words mean?

15 Karol Josef Wojtyla of Poland was quite influential in the fall of the Communist government in that Eastern Bloc country. Who is Karol Wojtyla?

16 Ruhollah Hendi played an important role in modern Middle East history. Who was Hendi?

17 On March 13, 1988, the world's longest—53.85 kilometers (a fraction more than 33.44 miles)—underwater tunnel was opened. In what country is this man-made wonder?

18 What was the Saur Revolution, and when did it take place?

19 In the 1988 Summer Olympics, which took place in South Korea, bowling made its debut as an exhibition sport. This is expected to lead to bowling becoming a full-fledged Olympic sport for the 1992 Games. In what country did bowling originate?

20 In April 1989 student demonstrations in Beijing, the capital of Mainland

China, were brutally suppressed, leading to hundreds of deaths. What were students protesting in the rallies that resulted in the Tiananmen Square massacre of June 3–4?

21 The current queen of England, as you probably know, is Elizabeth. What number follows her name?

22 Margaret Thatcher was the first prime minister of Great Britain in 160 years to be elected to a third term. Was Thatcher the first female British prime minister? And, if not, can you name the woman who was?

23 One of the most chilling attempts at censorship in this century was the death sentence with a $1 million reward issued by Iran's Ayatollah Khomeini for the murder of the author of a book Khomeini viewed as blasphemous to Islam. Name the author and the novel that Khomeini wanted destroyed.

24 By what name is 1979 Nobel Peace Prize winner Agnes Gonxha Bojaxhin world famous?

25 In 1989 the hit musical *Cats* set a record for longest-playing show in London history. Here's a three-part question for you. Name (a) the man who wrote the music, (b) the man who wrote the work from which the lyrics were taken, and (c) the name of that original work.

26 In the 1989 crumbling of the East European Communist states, can you name the country that first established diplomatic relations with the Vatican and also legalized the Catholic church?

27 In less than a decade (1997) the British lease giving them power over Hong Kong as a Crown Colony will end. How did Britain first gain colonial power over Hong Kong?

28 If you travel to Tokyo and ride on their subway system during *satowjin rasshu* (rush hour) you will probably encounter the *oshiya*. What are the oshiya?

29 In 1984 two bodyguards assassinated the prime minister they were assigned to protect. Who was the murdered government leader?

30 Few events in the collapse of the former Iron Curtain countries matched the tearing down of the Berlin Wall on November 9, 1989. Berlin, the capital of Nazi Germany, had been divided since the close of World War II. Was Berlin in East or West Germany?

31 One of the most newsworthy sports events in the 1980s was the boycott of the 1980 Summer Olympics. Here's a two-part question for you: (a) Where were those Games held, and (b) why was there a boycott?

32 On New Year's Day 1986, two TV broadcasts in two different countries made world history. What was historically unique about these broadcasts?

33 A hit record a few years back told the story of a man's lament for a woman trapped behind the Iron Curtain. In it, he opined: "You will never know anything about my home." The woman was painted in song as "counting ten tin soldiers in a row." Can you name the song and the artist who recorded it?

34 In 1982 Great Britain and Argentina fought a brief battle over territory claimed by both nations. What colony was involved in the dispute, which was won by the British forces?

35 On January 23, 1990, residents of Pitcairn Island burned a replica of an eighteenth-century British sailing vessel to celebrate the 200th anniversary of their ancestors settling there. Who were their ancestors?

36 Only one woman has ever ruled a Moslem country. Who was this prime minister?

37 Camp David has been a retreat for presidents since the days of Franklin Roosevelt. Its name was etched in history when the Camp David Accords were forged there in 1979.

Name the two nations involved in the Camp David Accords, and the leaders of those two nations who signed the treaty.

38 In 1990 *U.S. News & World Report* magazine published the list of the all-time best-selling paperback books. Only one author had two books listed in the Top Ten. Can you name the author and the books?

39 One of the terms that has cropped up over the last few years is "guerrilla mom." What is a guerrilla mom?

40 The Soviet Union is the largest country in the world. To give one some idea of its size, can you tell (guess?) how many time zones there are in the Soviet Union?

41 Only three foreign private citizens have ever been invited to address a joint session of the U.S. Congress. Can you name them?

42 The "European Economic Community" is a group comprised of twelve member-nations. By what more common name is it known?

43 Perhaps the most important news story to come out of the eighties was the spread of freedom through the Captive Nations (those East European countries formerly dominated by the Soviet Union). Of the following Eastern bloc nations (listed alphabetically)—Bulgaria, Czechoslovakia, East Germany, Hungary, Poland, and Romania—two do *not* border directly on Russia. Can you name either of the two?

44 In 1993, if all goes according to schedule, a project once held dear to Napoleon Bonaparte will become a reality. What was this Napoleonic goal?

Answers

① *Solidarnosc, or Solidarity, was the Polish union movement, led by Lech Walesa.*

② Jihad *means a holy war. It's taken from the Arabic word meaning struggle or strife.*

③ *It's the act of ritual suicide performed by a widow hurling herself on the funeral pyre of her late husband.*

④ *ROC means the Republic of China, which is located on Taiwan; PRC stands for the People's Republic of China, which is the Communist government on the mainland.*

⑤ *It's Spanish for counter-revolutionary. The Latin origin of the word means against, opposite, or opposing.*

⑥ *The word is derived from General Augusto Sandino, a Nicaraguan guerrilla who was executed by the national guard led by General Anastasio Somoza in 1934.*

⑦ *Karaoke (pronounced kah-rah-okay) means "empty orchestra" in its native Japanese. It's a lounge where the customers can select songs, usually on a laser disc, and get up before a microphone, and sing along.*

⑧ *Margaret Roberts is the maiden name of former Prime Minister Margaret Thatcher of Great Britain (1979–90).*

⑨ *The archipelago of some eighty islands was formerly known as the New Hebrides.*

⑩ *She was the first woman ever democratically elected to be a chief of state. Other women government leaders, such as former Prime Ministers Margaret Thatcher of Great Britain and Indira Gandhi of India, were selected by Parliaments rather than by direct popular election.*

⑪ Gone With the Wind.

⑫ *Boris Yeltsin.*

⑬ *The world's oldest republic is the Most Serene Republic of San Marino, which is surrounded by Italy. Anyone born there re-*

mains a citizen for life and can vote no matter where he or she may live.

(14) Glasnost *means open-ness or candor, and* perestroika *means restructuring.*

(15) *You probably know him better by his adopted name: Pope John Paul II, who in 1978 became the first non-Italian pope in 455 years.*

(16) *This is the name the late Iranian despot Ayatollah Ruhollah Khomeini was given at birth (1900). He changed it in 1930, based on his birthplace, Khomein.*

(17) *Seikan Tunnel links Japan's main island, Honshu, with the island of Hokkaido.*

(18) *This is the name used in Soviet-occupied Kabul, Afghanistan, for the Communist takeover of that nation's government in the late 1970s.*

(19) *Ancient Germany was the birthplace of bowling. The early Dutch settlers brought it to the New World.*

(20) *They were mourning the death of Hu Yaobang. Yaobang had been ousted as Communist party secretary two years earlier.*

㉑ *The current queen is Elizabeth II. The only other Elizabeth, Elizabeth I, the Virgin Queen, reigned from 1558 to 1603.*

㉒ *Margaret Thatcher was Great Britain's first female prime minister.*

㉓ *Khomeini's target in the 1989 declaration was Salman Rushdie, author of* The Satanic Verses. *Although Khomeini died that same year, the assassination threat continues.*

㉔ *You know her as Mother Teresa of Calcutta. Born in Skopje, Macedonia, in 1910, Mother Teresa became a Roman Catholic nun and founded the Order of the Missionaries of Charity.*

㉕ *(a) Andrew Lloyd Webber set to music the lyrics from (b) T.S. Eliot's work (c)* Old Possum's Book of Practical Cats.

㉖ *Poland was the first former Iron Curtain country to recognize the Vatican.*

㉗ *The island of Hong Kong was ceded to Britain as part of the Treaty of Nanking (1842), ending the Opium War.*

㉘ *The* oshiya *are pushers. Their job is to push commuters onto the subway cars, packing them to their capacity.*

㉙ *It was India's Prime Minister Indira Gandhi (1917–84). In 1991, Mrs.*

Gandhi's son, Rajiv Gandhi, suffered a similar fate albeit not at the hands of his bodyguards.

㉚ *Berlin was within the borders of East Germany.*

㉛ *(a) Led by the United States, sixty-two nations boycotted the Moscow Games, because of (b) the Soviet invasion of Afghanistan.*

㉜ *President Ronald Reagan appeared on a special broadcast beamed to the Soviet Union, and Soviet President Mikhail Gorbachev's message was aired in the United States.*

㉝ *It was* Nikita *by Elton John. By the way, a Russian perfectionist-friend observed that Nikita is a man's name, but, who cares, the thought was what counted.*

㉞ *It was the Falkland Islands, some 250 miles off the Argentine coast. Both nations had claimed possession of the Falklands dating back to 1833, but they were under British control both prior to and after the conflict.*

㉟ *Their ancestors were the famed mutineers immortalized in* Mutiny on the Bounty.

㊱ *In 1988 Benazir Bhutto was elected prime minister of Pakistan. Her father, Zulfikar Ali Bhutto, had been president of Pakistan from 1970 to 1977. The father-daughter team were ill-fated. In 1979 he was hanged on charges of complicity in a political murder, and she was dismissed from her prime ministerial post in 1990 for alleged corruption and nepotism.*

㊲ *Menachem Begin of Israel and Anwar Sadat of Egypt placed their signatures on the document. While it was drawn at Camp David, the signing took place March 26, 1979, in Washington.*

㊳ *Number Four on the list was George Orwell's* 1984; *his other antitotalitarian novel,* Animal Farm, *ranked Number Seven.*

㊴ *In Red China, with its compulsory abortion laws aimed at stemming population growth, a guerrilla mom is an expectant mother who goes into hiding to avoid losing her child.*

㊵ *The Soviet Union extends over eleven time zones.*

㊶ *In 1824 the Marquis de Lafayette, who was invaluable to the colonists in the Revolutionary War became the first. In 1989 Poland's Solidarity leader, Lech Walesa, became the second. And, in 1990 Nelson Mandela, the South African who has led the drive against apartheid, became the third.*

㊷ *You probably know it more as the European Common Market.*

④③ *Bulgaria and East Germany do not share a border with the Soviet Union.*

④④ *The French emperor longed to see a tunnel connecting France and England. The over-budget Chunnel, as it is called, is slated for a grand opening on June 15, 1993.*